THE AMAZING

600 CALORIE

MODEL'S DIET

Bunny Yeager

Photographs by Harry W. Schaefer

PARKER PUBLISHING COMPANY, INC.

West Nyack, New York

Library of Congress Cataloging in Publication Data

Yeager, Bunny.
    The amazing 600 calorie model's diet.

    Includes index.
    1. Low-calorie diet.   2. Food–Caloric content–
Tables. I. Title. II. Title: Model's diet.
RM222.2.Y4   613.2′5   79-27185
ISBN 0-13-023770-1

Printed in the United States of America

A Word
from the Author

This book is for every woman who feels that she is overweight, whether it be by 5 pounds or 50 pounds. Even if you are a diet dropout, I can help you. Every woman has a great potential for being a beauty and she should work toward that goal as completely as she is able. One of the easiest ways to become more beautiful is to lose any excess weight you may have accumulated over the years. A slender body is healthy and youthful looking.

It gives me great pleasure to share with you the dieting secrets used by models to lose weight quickly, safely and permanently. Having been a beauty queen and a fashion and photographer's model for many years prior to starting my photographic career, I was acutely aware of how important it was to be able to keep my weight stable and unfluctuating, so that I would always be able to wear the size clothing that was noted on my model's composite.

Later on, when I became a glamour photographer shooting covers and centerfolds for magazines like *Playboy*, I was even more aware of what a few extra pounds on a pretty girl can mean as to whether her photographs would be accepted or rejected. Before one gets an assignment of this type, test shots have to be made of the model showing all her angles, both good and bad, so that it can be determined if her attractive points outnumber her faults. There were a number of times when I was told by an editor or art director, "If she can lose about 10 pounds in the next couple of weeks, we may be able to use her, but she is definitely too chunky right now."

This meant that the girl had to lose her excess weight fast before the editor changed his mind about considering her. If she took too long, there were other girls "waiting in the wings" to take her place.

I've helped many models reduce and control their weights by using this diet, and I feel that it is the best one if you are looking for the quickest means of eliminating fat.

For any weight control program to succeed it must begin with a common sense education about nutrition, exercise and what made you fat in the first place. I've done all the research and experimenting. I've counted the calories and planned your menus for you. You have nothing to do but follow the information in this book and you can't help but lose that unwanted weight.

I've provided you with valuable hints for staying on your diet. You can learn how to avoid fatigue while dieting and find out how to enjoy your life more than you have in the past. Guidance is given for improving your looks so that you'll appear prettier and slimmer while you are still trying to lose that weight.

I won't promise that you will have more sex appeal by following my diet, but when you begin to feel more alive and healthier, it will show all over in the way you walk, talk and think. That in itself can make anyone sexier.

My *Amazing 600 Calorie Model's Diet* has been successful for everyone who's tried it and it can be for you, too. This will be the last time you go on a diet. Believe this and let me take you by the hand step by step toward becoming the slim beauty you know is hiding within you.

Before starting this diet (as with any diet) do check with your doctor to make sure you have no medical problems other than poor eating and exercise habits. I'm sure he'll give his approval and you can start right in at once. The day you start your diet will be the beginning of a more exciting, happier, healthier life. Think about that and believe in it and you will find it coming true. Remember, you're in charge of your body and you control what it does and what it is. It will be what you make it. Let me help you.

Bunny Yeager

Contents

**15. The Charming New You
and How to Stay That Way**...................... 210

The Right Way to Celebrate... Rewarding Yourself...
Letting Others See You... Making Yourself Good Company... So Now You Want to Be a Model!

1

The Model's Way to Lose Weight:
A New Approach
to Weight Control

I am sure you realize that professional models must be both slender and healthy. In addition to looking great, every model must be healthy, for modeling certainly requires stamina.

Today, the average teenage girl dreams about becoming a professional model, just as 40 or 50 years ago, every teenage girl used to fantasize about going to Hollywood and becoming a movie star. A girl may spend her time reading fashion magazines and clipping out pictures of a particular idol so that she can imitate her look as accurately as possible. Professional models are held in high esteem not only by teenage girls, but by all women, including career girls, housewives and older women who never had the chance to pursue such a glamorous career when they were young.

Not only do successful models make a lot of money, but they also represent perfection in beauty and charm. Only one girl in a thousand is pretty enough to succeed as a professional model.

Professional models are not born—they are made and developed. Of course, a model has to start out with some natural beauty of her own, but then she must learn correct posture, showroom walking, the use of cosmetics, how to dress and many other related skills. All models have some imperfections and must find ways to disguise and hide them. But one thing is certain: Every model must have a slender body.

You may not want to become a professional model, but maybe you think it would be fun to look like one. It might even improve your love life!

TAKING CARE OF YOURSELF

If you are married, you should know that, as much as you feel obligated to care for your family, you also have an obligation to yourself, that of reaching your potential in life and realizing just how beautiful you can be. Today, the average married woman is not only the housekeeper, cook, laundress, nursemaid, seamstress and chauffeur, but she may also be a part-time or even full-time breadwinner. You do yourself (and your family) an injustice if you do not take care of yourself and be the person you know you can and should be.

You can do this by losing your excess weight as soon as possible. This will not only make you look better, but you'll be healthier, enjoying new energy and interest in life.

THE IMPORTANCE OF WEIGHT TO A MODEL

As I said before, every model must start out in her career with a slender body, but that doesn't mean she doesn't worry about getting fat. The way her body looks and how much it weighs is as important to her as the makeup on her face. A model has to keep her size consistent. She cannot be a size 7 this week and a size 10 three weeks from now. An agency never sends a model out for an interview with a client unless she is the exact size that he requests. Many times a model is hired just on the basis of a client seeing her photographs at the agency. You can readily understand why a model has to look exactly like her photographs all the time. A client's time is valuable and he isn't going to be too happy if he has been fooled into thinking that a model is anything other than what appears in her model's composite or portfolio. If this situation should occur several times with the same agency, the client may discontinue dealing with that agency. A model doesn't win any popularity contests with her agent when this happens.

Models are not perfect. They gain weight when they eat too much, just like the rest of us. So, like everyone else, they have to diet when they accumulate a few extra pounds. The only difference is that they don't have all the time in the world to do it. As soon as they realize that they are heavier than they should be, they must do something about it fast. If they procrastinate for too long, they may be ex-models in a very short time.

HOW KATHLEEN V. PROTECTED HER CAREER

Kathleen V. was a popular model until she began to gain too much weight. She soon weighed 125 pounds, and realized that, for a girl of her height (5'2"), that made her about 10 to 15 pounds overweight. Kathleen knew she'd have to diet, and followed her diet strictly at first. She lost 4 pounds the first week, went out to dinner to celebrate, and gained back 3 of the 4 pounds she had lost. Even worse, for the next couple of days she was so upset that she couldn't pick up her dieting where she had left off. By the third day, however, she knew that her career was at stake, and began her diet all over again. This time she stuck with it, and two weeks later, she was down to 110 pounds, the proper weight for her. Now Kathleen knows that whenever her eating gets out of control for even one day, she must go back on her diet to stabilize her desired weight.

After all, the people who hire models have a choice of many girls, each one as pretty as the other. It doesn't make any difference to these photographers or fashion designers which one they use. They just want the job done with the best model they can find. If you don't shape up, there's always another model just as pretty as you are, waiting in the wings to take your place. If excess weight causes you to be passed over once, it is that much harder to be accepted again for modeling work even after you correct your weight problem.

Models have discovered that, to lose weight fast, you must use a Spartan diet—almost a starvation diet—and follow it strictly for a while. Because the weight loss results come quickly, models don't have to stay on their diets for very long, so they can put up with it until they get results.

HOW I DEVELOPED THE AMAZING 600 CALORIE MODEL'S DIET

Many overweight models have come to me for advice on dieting. The 600 Calorie Model's Diet evolved because of my own dieting experiences and what I learned from interviewing models who had lost weight successfully in a short period of time.

Nobody has failed to lose weight by following this diet and all stayed in good health while they were on the diet. It is amazing how little food we need for our bodies to function properly. No other method will help you to lose weight quite as fast as this, except for a total fast. A complete fast can be all right for a few days, but anyone who tries to fast for longer should be under the care of a physician or in a hospital. By lowering your calorie intake to 600 calories per day, you are cutting down tremendously, but you are still getting enough nutrition to keep your body going so that you can work and play without fatigue. As I said before, it's not exactly fun, but it works!

If beautiful models can diet, so can you. If beautiful models can do without a lot of food, so can you. If beautiful models can lose weight quickly on this diet, so can you. Models *have* to. Don't *you* have to, too?

AVOIDING DANGEROUS WEIGHT LOSS METHODS

There is no *easy* way to lose weight. Dieting Americans are perhaps the most gullible people in the world. We do not want to face up to the fact that there is no instant, magical way to get rid of unwanted fat. We want to believe those misleading advertisements that promise quick results with the use of pills, magic formulas, vibrators or other devices. Commercial liquid diet foods may produce results, but at what price to your nutrition? Eating diet cookies or puddings three times a day might sound attractive to a person who craves sweets, but imagine how boring that can become. No wonder people don't stay on diets for very long. They can be so unbearably boring!

Diet drugs are not the answer either. Congressional hearings a number of years ago spotlighted the potential hazards of using drugs for dieting. Testimony from thousands of women disclosed that many of them were taking pills without proper medical supervision. Pills were being passed around from friend to friend without prescriptions and without these women knowing what they were actually taking or what harm they might be doing to their bodies. Only because many deaths occurred as a result of this were any investigations conducted.

There are at least 10,000 "fat doctors" in the United States, who see at least 10,000,000 patients. These are doctors who specialize in handling cases of obesity by operating clinics where many patients can be seen and treated quickly. They spend only a few minutes with each patient, either to praise them for having lost some weight since the last visit, or to chastise them for having gained weight. These clinics see a steady flow of fat people who are eager to pay whatever price is asked in order to get the "magic pills" that will enable them to lose their excess fat quickly and easily.

The most commonly used diet drugs are amphetamines. It is true that they will reduce appetite, but there are unfavorable side effects. Furthermore, the effect they produce lasts for only a few weeks unless the dosage is increased. Drugs such as these can cause high blood pressure or palpitations of the heart, so it is not advisable to take large doses.

Diuretics are sometimes used in a weight loss program, but the weight loss that results is because of a decrease in water, not fat reduction. As soon as the patient stops taking the diuretic, his weight increases as more water is retained normally in his system.

MECHANICAL DEVICES

Overweight Americans spend over $100,000,000 per year on mechanical devices that claim to reduce fat with effortless exercise. Naturally, this appeals to those dieters who are lazy, but it is effort that makes exercise beneficial in the first place!

One electrical exerciser has pads which are placed on the thighs and a belt which can be placed on the hips, waist or abdomen. The muscles are contracted involuntarily by electrical impulses shot through the body. This can be dangerous if the current enters the heart at a critical time in its cycle and upsets its rhythm, which could happen if the pads are placed too near the heart or if current should leak from faulty wiring.

Another device is a vinyl-coated belt weighted with lead pellets, which is worn around the waist as you go about your daily tasks. According to the manufacturer, the belts work on the weight-resistance theory. A muscle pushes against the weight it is carrying and, in doing so, is supposed to become firmer. I've never heard of anyone losing any weight by wearing one of these belts.

Department stores and mail order catalogs sell hip vibrating machines. A belt is placed around the hips or buttocks and a motor manipulates the belt so that your fat can be taken off by shaking or vibrating it. Of course, the fat doesn't actually go anywhere; you're still as heavy as you were before you started!

HEALTH SPAS

Health spas can be useful in helping you to lose weight because it is encouraging to have company when you exercise. Unfortunately, most of those shiny chrome and leather exercise machines in the spas and reducing salons are worthless because you use so few of your muscles to operate them. Psychologically, they can be relaxing, but that's all. You'll never lose weight by using them. If you go to a spa or reducing salon, head for the machines that require some effort to operate. The ones with pulleys and weights are best, since you can increase the amounts or the number of weights as you progress.

Some form of exercise should be part of every reducing plan, and fortunately for you, none of these machines, devices or gadgets is really necessary. All you really need are your own body and some enthusiasm. I'll explain later just how easy it can be.

There have always been fad diets, but I don't know of any diet, no matter how popular, that is as quick and effective as this Amazing 600 Calorie Model's Diet. Most of the women reading this book will have tried one or more of the many fad diets and discovered that they just don't do the job, Even if you have tried a number of diets and have failed to lose weight permanently, don't despair.

You may have chosen diets that were wrong for you, or there may have been other reasons why you might have failed at a particular time in your life. Maybe you felt you just didn't have the willpower to stick to the diet for long enough. Maybe troubles in your personal life or your working conditions were taking too much out of you. Maybe your motivation was wrong, or maybe at that time you just didn't want to lose those excess pounds badly enough to let any diet work.

When you compare yourself to a model and start the Amazing 600 Calorie Model's Diet, you set up rather high goals for yourself, but there is no reason why you have to fail this time. And why shouldn't you use a professional model as your example to follow? Why bother copying the girl in the next office or your neighbor down the street? Try to make yourself look like the best—like the professional model!

Look through the fashion magazines for a model whom you feel you resemble. Study her look, how she does her hair and makeup. All through your dieting period, think of yourself as that model. Make believe that you *are* a model who has just happened to let her weight go for a while, and now you are just getting yourself back into shape.

Please take me seriously and don't laugh when I suggest this, even though it may be hard now for you to identify yourself with any kind of model. Look in the mirror and check out your bone structure, your eyes, your hair. Surely you can find one girl in one of the magazines who expresses your own image. Don't think about your body now, but only about your facial features. Many magazines feature one model in several outfits or, if the model is really popular, you will find her in several magazine layouts at the same time. Start by doing this and you'll begin to see yourself as a different person.

The purpose of the Amazing 600 Calorie Model's Diet is not only for you to lose your excess weight, but also to attain the beauty, charm and poise a professional model must have if she is to be successful in her career. This doesn't mean that you should think you could become a professional model after completing this diet; it only means that I think you should make the most of what you have, giving more pleasure to yourself and to the people around you.

2

Let's Look You Over
It's Never Too Late!

Sooner or later, almost everyone needs to go on a reducing diet to lose some excess pounds, whether to improve their health or merely for esthetic reasons. To me, both factors are equally important. I want to keep my good health and my good looks for as long as I am able. If this is within my control, why not?

HOW YOU CAN "PUT OFF" AGING

Fatty deposits on the body, in the form of pot bellies, double chins, saggy arms and rippled legs, always tend to make you look much older than you are. A slim figure represents youth, and the longer you can present a svelte, trim figure to your "public," the longer you will "put off" aging. A slim figure is a healthier figure. Why carry around excess weight that makes it more difficult to get around, leaving you huffing and puffing for breath? Why overtax your heart? Fat people court heart attacks, diabetes and other related diseases. Anyone who cares about herself at all wants to preserve and take care of her body and present as good a physical image as possible. You are given one body and it has to last a lifetime. What are you doing to help? Are you part of the solution or part of the problem? What are you doing to take care of your body and see to it that it lasts a long time and looks as good as it can? People who let themselves gain ugly pounds give the following impressions to those around them:

- They lack discipline and self-control.
- They don't care about their health.
- They don't care about how they appear to others.

People who gain excess weight can be compared to a run-down neighborhood. Would you let the paint peel off your house and the weeds grow as high as the windows? Your body is the most important thing you will ever own and control. Your body is you, and your most important goal should be to take good care of it and maintain it as well as you possibly can. To maintain a fancy car or house may require more money than to maintain an economy automobile or inexpensive frame dwelling, but taking care of your body needn't entail any great expense. The average person can do it just as well as one who is wealthy. The important thing is to know how to do it. Before I tell you how, let's see just what we have to work with. Let's take a look at your body.

So that we can best determine just how much figure improvement you must accomplish with your dieting and exercise, let's evaluate the raw material you have to work with. Your physical self may not be as bad as you think.

We are so occupied with slimness in our culture that people sometimes equate a near-emaciated body with an idea of beauty. Do you really need to reduce? You should not try to copy the ultra-thin high fashion model. Being too thin is not healthy, for it lowers your body's resistance to disease. The kind of model you will want to pattern your body after is the illustrative photographer's model, the girl you see advertising suntan lotion, a soft drink, a shampoo or a breakfast food. She is slender, but not thin—well-rounded, but without bulges.

YOUR SELF-EXAMINATION

You'll need a full-length mirror to examine yourself. Get undressed down to your bra and panties. Face the mirror, legs together, arms at your sides. You don't like what you see, do you?

Now turn to the side and look yourself over. If you have a triple mirror so that you can see behind you, observe your back as well. Pick out your most objectionable fault. Is it your protruding stomach? A "pot belly" announces to the world that you're overweight. If your stomach didn't stick out so much, people might think of you as "pleasingly plump" instead of rotund. This is the biggest trouble area for everyone and the place you must work on as soon as possible. Look at yourself some more. Turn around again, this way and that. Look at those lumps, ripples and rolls of fat. Here is a body all stretched out of shape by years of poor eating habits and excesses. It didn't get that way overnight, so resign yourself to the fact that you will not correct it overnight, either. You have a lot of work to do.

Take a piece of notepaper and write down all of the faults you can find with your figure. Note the things you want to work on and correct as you lose weight. You'll find specific exercises for particular figure problems in Chapter 13, and later you'll want to copy the names of these exercises next to your figure faults.

USING A SCALE EFFECTIVELY

Don't start any reducing plan until you get a scale for weighing yourself. This is very important. The best time for you to "weigh in" is the first thing in the morning. The reason I suggest this time of day is because it has been discovered that you weigh less in the morning than at any other time.

I want you to weigh yourself every day from now on, and always at the same time. Wear as little clothing as possible when you are on the scale, and, of course, no shoes. You should record your weight each day so that you can keep tabs on your progress, or your regression. I've found that a steno pad is handy for this purpose, because you can not only record your daily weight, but you can also use the rest of the space on each page to record what you eat during that day, as well as the calories in what you eat.

You should put the date and your weight at the top of the page. If you want to keep a record of your measurements, put them down too, but you don't have to measure yourself again until you have lost at least 3 to 5 pounds.

Marie McR. had never kept any sort of record of her weight or measurements, even though she worked as a model. In fact, whenever the 5′ 8″ beauty was asked what she weighed, she said she didn't know. But suddenly her clothes began to fit too snugly around the waist and hips, and Marie realized she was becoming overweight. When she finally weighed herself, she got a shock—she weighed 145 pounds. According to the height/weight charts, Marie should have weighed about 130 to 135 pounds at most. Marie immediately put herself on the Amazing 600 Calorie Model's Diet, followed it strictly, and lost 11 pounds in ten days. Now she weighs herself every single day.

When you measure yourself, the spots to measure are: bust, waist, stomach, hips, lower hips, upper thighs and upper arms. Measure your bust while wearing your best-fitting bra. Place the measuring tape around the largest part, making sure that the tape doesn't slip down in the back. The waist, of course, is measured at its narrowest point. Do not pull in tightly. The stomach is measured at the largest part. Find your hip bone to measure your hips. It will be about 7 inches down from your waist, if you cannot feel it readily. The lower hips include the buttocks as well, at the fullest point. Place the measuring tape around your thighs until they measure the largest. Record that figure. Do the same thing with your upper arms. Never pull the tape too tightly when measuring your body. You may want to draw a box around your measurements with a red marker so that you can find the information more easily for reference when you are taking your measurements the next time. The second time you measure yourself (after some weight loss), draw a chart like this on a piece of notepaper:

	Last Time	This Time	Inches Lost
Bust			
Waist			
Stomach			
Hips			
Lower Hips			
Upper Thighs			
Upper Arms			

The third time you measure yourself (after another weight loss), add another column: *Total Inches Lost*. This record-keeping should help spur you on to your goal.

On the upper left-hand side of the same page where you have listed the date, weight and measurements, write in the figure *600*. During the day, as you eat various foods, you will not only list the food and the amount that you eat, but you will also list its calorie count, subtracting the amounts from the 600 starting figure. Here's the way the beginning of your page might look:

Date:_____	135 lbs.

Calories	Food
600	
−80	1 hardboiled egg
520	
−33	1 tomato
487	
−18	6 Oysterette crackers
469	

When you have run out of the calories in your "calorie bank," you must stop eating for the day. Fortunately, I have prepared some sample menus for each day of your diet so that you will not run out of ideas for the kinds and amounts of food you can eat. The secret of success in this particularly strict diet is to plan ahead. Never give yourself a chance to wonder about what you are going to eat next. Your choice of food must be there when you need it, and it must have the calorie count you can afford to spend. Try to follow my menus as closely as you can, without substitution, for best results.

When you reach the end of the month, make a note of the following records and draw a red box around the information so you can find it the next month.

Weight Today:_____

Highest Weight This Month:_____

Lowest Weight This Month:_____

Difference in Weight Between Highest and Lowest Weight:_____

(Eventually we want to keep this figure as low as possible so that your weight will not be fluctuating drastically.)

You'll keep these records at the end of every month of your diet. Yes, I did say "every month." You are not going to lose all the weight you have gained in a matter of weeks. It is going to take months. If you have 50 or more pounds to lose, it could take as long as a year to do it. Let me remind you again: You did not put on that weight in a couple of weeks. It accumulated over the years. Realistically, then, you must stay on your diet for several months, allowing for times when you slide back to your old eating habits and have to recover from them.

The first step in preparing for any diet is to acknowledge that you do indeed have a problem. That's why I wanted you to examine yourself very carefully in the mirror and pick out all the bad things about your figure. Too often we look in a mirror and see what we want to see and not what is actually there. I want you to see yourself as others see you. I want you to say to yourself, "I don't want to be like this anymore. I want to find out why I'm like this. I need help. I want to do whatever it takes to become normal again. I'm ready to start a reducing diet and stick to it, no matter how long it takes."

By saying this to yourself, you have accepted the fact that you definitely have a problem and want to find a solution. The more you can look at yourself and remind yourself about your problem, the more you will stick to your diet and succeed in losing the weight you have to lose.

Since you can't go around looking at yourself in the mirror all day, there is another way you can remind yourself as often as you like that you have to lose weight *now* and must stick to your diet until all the weight is gone. That's by using a photograph. I don't mean this to be used as a punishment, but only as a reminder that tells you, "This is how I look to other people. Do I really want to go through life looking like this?"

Put on a bathing suit or a leotard and have a friend take a photograph of you from the front, from the side and from the back. A Polaroid camera is great for this because you won't have to get the film developed. If you don't have a Polaroid camera, then any camera will do. If you're too embarrassed to take the film for developing, ask your friend to do it.

Carry these photographs with you at all times and take them out and look at them whenever you even feel slightly hungry, or whenever you need a boost in your willpower to continue your positive thoughts on dieting. As you lose weight, the photos will still be helpful because you'll gain an even stronger determination to lose more so that you don't ever look like that again. Yes, you'll do anything to keep from looking like that, you'll even stay on your Spartan diet of 600 calories a day!

You have no idea what satisfaction you will feel when your diet is over and you can have photographs made of yourself that you will want to show to anyone and everyone. Always keep those "before" pictures so that you never ever fall into bad eating habits again. Not only will you find joy in looking at the "after" pictures, but you'll be buoyed up with pleasure every time you pass a store window and view your new slim reflection or every time you put on your clothes and they fit. You'll have no more popping buttons or zippers that won't close. You'll have the feeling that your life is finally "in order."

Now back to the problem at hand. You do still have a long way to go, and dreaming about the future won't hurt, but you must face reality and get started on your plan.

Now that we know all the bad news, let's find out some good news. Take another look in your full-length mirror. Tell me what you see that is *good* about yourself, and don't be modest. Let's make a list. How's your skin? Can we say you have good skin? Put that down as number 1 on your list. Look at your hair. Would you say you're proud of the way your hair looks? Then list that as number 2. What do you consider to be your best feature? Your eyes? List that as number 3. You have long nails? Add that to your list. Whatever you see about yourself that you feel is good or even passable, put it all down on your "Good Features" list. I don't care how hopeless you think you are, you certainly have a number of good points, and I want you to remember what they are as you diet. List all of the physical attributes first—the things you can actually see. Now make a second list of all the good things about yourself that you cannot see, but that are a part of your true inner self. Which of these are your best features? Do people say you have a good personality? List that. Do you help people whenever you can? That's another plus in your favor. Why am I asking you to make these lists? Because I want you to have a high self-esteem. It's easy to feel depressed and moody when you're on a diet and you see mostly the things that are wrong with you instead of the good things.

Look at this list as often as you need to if you become depressed during your diet. Take pride in what you are. You are a worthwhile human being and you are going to be even better when you are through with your diet. You should be able to feel yourself getting better daily. Think well of yourself and others will do the same. When the people you come into contact with find out that you are dieting, they will respect you for it and be happy for you. They realize that it takes a lot of willpower for an overweight person to stick to any kind of diet. Most people have tried dieting at some time in their lives, so they know what you are going through. You are not alone. If you know what your problems are and how to correct them, and if you are doing something to eliminate them, then you are well on your way to being a better person, not only physically, but emotionally as well. Think how proud you'll be that you were able to practice self-control, perhaps for the first time in your life. Give yourself a big smile every time you look in a mirror from now on. You're really "somebody" because you're in control of your life. Your stomach is no longer ruling your brain. You are going to determine just what you will be in the future: a fantastic individual!

3

How to Motivate Yourself
to Reduce

Why do you overeat? If you are like most people, you eat too much not because you are always hungry, but because of an emotional need. You overeat because you are bored, or nervous, or lonely, or depressed. Most people get bored at one time or another, but certain age groups and certain personality types are more prone to boredom than others. City people are bored more often than country people, extroverts suffer more than introverts, and most mothers who are confined for long periods to the exclusive company of small children are likely to experience boredom.

Depressed, unhappy people tend to eat too much. Overweight people tend to blame their condition on whatever failure they have experienced in life. This is rarely entirely true, although being fat can understandably aggravate and perpetuate feelings of failure.

HOW TO KEEP FROM BECOMING BORED

Boredom seems to set in whenever we no longer find pleasure in our own thoughts and fantasies, when we become too dependent on external stimuli and then find ourselves removed from them. How can we dispel boredom? We can seek out other people, ideally men and women whose backgrounds or temperaments are different from our own.

Make a friend of someone who grew up in another country. If you grew up in a middle-class or well-to-do neighborhood, make friends with someone who had a more deprived childhood. If you are by nature very quiet, find a stimulating companion who has a "devil-may-care" attitude about life. If you are a voluble, life-of-the-party person, seek out a conscientious, low-key type of individual. Someone much older or someone much younger, someone more intellectual or less intellectual than you are will bring you new experiences and pick you up out of your doldrums.

Reading fiction can help, too. The more unreal it is, the better. Music can help you fantasize and excite your interest if you explore sounds that are less familiar to you. Going back to nature can give you a fresh look at life. Just hiking through the woods, going fishing or taking a canoe ride may help your perspective. Decorating can be an effective antidote for boredom for most women. Clothing, too, can serve the same purpose if you are able to sew and create original ideas from old patterns. Hobbies are only good if you truly enjoy them, instead of using them as "busy" work. Remember that if you get bored, you are going to eat more, so start thinking now about what you will do before the symptoms of boredom start to set in on you.

HOW EATING CAN CAUSE DEPRESSION

Depression often triggers overeating. This in turn makes you more depressed, and the vicious cycle never seems to end. Certain foods can make you depressed when you eat them, so to avoid feeling "down," cut out sweet foods like candy, cakes, cookies, desserts and soft drinks. Foods such as these cause the body's blood sugar level to drop and that puts you in a low, bad mood. You do need carbohydrates, but it's best to get them the natural way from fresh vegetables, fruit and unprocessed whole grain foods. Also keep away from junk foods such as potato chips, ice cream, colas and pastries. Try to eat foods that are rich in potassium such as bananas, oranges, leafy vegetables and lean meat. Potassium helps overcome anxiety.

You can keep stress and nervousness under control by taking a break from your regular routines. Sometimes you set too tight a schedule to follow, not leaving enough time for the things you feel you must accomplish throughout the day.

If you find you have several difficult tasks to do in one day, choose an easy one to do just before them. If you're a "morning person" (like I am) put the most annoying and hardest tasks into your morning schedule. If you're the kind of person who just can't wake up until you've had two or three cups of coffee, then do your easy, routine jobs first and put off the harder or more disagreeable ones until later.

Success or failure in losing weight may well depend on your whole attitude toward life—whether you have self-confidence, satisfaction with your work, a feeling of being loved, security in your family and a good outlook about social and everyday relationships.

WHY DO YOU WANT TO REDUCE?

The answer is not so simple. Everyone knows it is bad to be overweight because it is a threat to health as well as a social handicap. But why do *you* want to reduce, and what are you trying to accomplish? Do you have some grandiose unattainable goal that has little hope of success even if you do lose weight, or are you realistic in wanting to be slim? Don't set yourself up for frustration and eventual failure. Dieting is lonely. Most of the time, even people who are close to you don't know how to help you, and many times they even hinder your progress without ever knowing it. A dieter doesn't want to be reminded about how heavy she is, so it is helpful when people *don't* ask, "How much did you lose?" You're trying to forget you were heavier and they keep bringing it up. Mothers and husbands are not on our side when they keep insisting that we "eat something right now" or else we're bound to get sick. The friends and relatives who are most helpful to dieters are those who just leave us alone and accept what we are doing as what we have chosen to do.

NO ONE CAN DIET FOR YOU

You have to diet for yourself and yourself alone. Why? Because if you diet for "someone else," there may come a day when you will want to punish that person. How better to do it than to overeat again and become fat or even fatter? You may be saying to yourself, "I'm too mature for that. I'd never do such a stupid thing." But, are any of us so mature that we don't act like little children at times when things don't go exactly the way we think they should?

WHY CINDY P. FOUND DIETING DIFFICULT

Cindy P. went on a diet to lose weight when she fell in love with Steve, the young man who worked in the next office. She saw him at lunch every day in the bank's cafeteria. He was pleasant enough to her and she knew that they would make a good match if only he would ask her out. She also knew that she was too fat for anyone as good-looking as Steve to think about dating. But if she lost weight he'd notice her. He'd have to fall in love with her. Cindy knew that she was basically attractive because everyone told her so, even though she was fat, so Steve would have to fall in love with her when she got thin. Well, it took Cindy 8 months to get back into a size 7 dress and lose all the excess weight she had put on.

Sure enough, one day Steve did notice that she was more than just an office fixture and asked her out to dinner. That first evening with Steve was heaven. Everything went just the way she had fantasized in her daydreams. Cindy was walking on air. This state of affairs lasted for several months. Then a new girl came to work in the office where Steve was employed.

That weekend Steve was rather cool toward Cindy. He suggested that they both should start dating other people to make sure they were really in love. Cindy wanted no part of this, but she had no choice. As her dates with Steve became more and more infrequent, Cindy began to eat more, even when she wasn't really hungry. She didn't want to date anyone else; she only wanted Steve. But there were those lonely nights that left a void in her life.

One night Cindy drowned her loneliness in a bag of corn chips and a six-pack of beer. Her situation changed. Soon she began to buy a half-gallon of ice cream every few nights and devour the whole thing while she watched TV. In only a short time, Cindy ballooned back up to her old fat self and became depressed and withdrawn. Only after a number of visits to a sympathetic psychiatrist did Cindy discover what her problem was. She was trying to punish Steve for leaving her. She also learned what she had to do about her problem in order to lose weight sensibly. Cindy had to want to lose weight for herself, instead of for Steve or any other person.

WHAT TYPE OF DIET IS RIGHT FOR YOU?

You must decide whether you can adjust your everyday living to the demands of a reducing diet. Are you willing, for your own sake and your body's sake, to make the sacrifices involved? Because your emotions play such a large part in successful dieting, you cannot make yourself stay on a fad diet. If you don't really want to be thin, boredom and nervousness will set in, making it hard for you to concentrate on normal, everyday things such as office work or even taking care of your house.

Staying slim is a lifelong task for every overweight individual. You have to learn new eating habits and follow them even after your diet is over. Otherwise your lost weight will return and it will come back in much less time than the first time you gained it. You can't make yourself live forever on a strict reducing diet of constant self-denial without ruining your physical health and giving yourself serious psychological problems.

WHAT DOES FOOD MEAN TO YOU?

Many people eat when they feel lonely or sad, others because they are starved for affection and still others to relieve tension. In effect, the food is saying to them, "I love you and care about you." Food helps them to alleviate their feelings of depression. To go on a diet means you have to deprive yourself of pleasures you normally enjoy. It's almost like losing a loved one. People who are depressed to begin with will experience even more depression when they start a diet, so psychologically one has to evaluate whether it is better to be happy though fat, or to go on a diet and risk experiencing trying periods of depression that may cause even more problems. It is a good idea to talk this over with your doctor when you consult him about starting your reducing diet, as he may be able to prescribe medication to help you get through the beginning of your diet.

HOW AL B. CONQUERED HIS WEIGHT PROBLEM

Al B. was a 42-year-old politician who weighed roughly about 300 pounds. He had always been grossly obese ever since his teens. After a doctor examined him for insurance purposes, he advised Al to lose 100 pounds, or he would not be able to take out additional life insurance. Al was shocked because he claimed he felt healthy, but eventually he accepted the diagnosis and begged the doctor to hospitalize him and help him to lose the required weight. The doctor agreed and in seemingly no time at all, Al was down to his "normal" weight of 180 pounds. Al was happy about losing all this weight because a new election was coming up and he felt overjoyed at the thought of having new photographs taken for his campaign posters. Then something happened and Al became depressed. It started when Al was making his round of political speeches. Instead of being elated and in high spirits, he started to lose confidence in himself and dreaded his personal appearances. His massive figure had always seemed to be a symbol of authority and power, and now with his normal body he began to feel small, weak and unimportant. He asked the doctor to prescribe sleeping pills for him because he couldn't sleep at night, and tranquilizers for the day so that he could face his audiences again. Whether it was his lack of confidence or just that his opponent was a better man, he lost the election and the next day he was found unconscious by his wife, a victim of drug overdose due to depression. He was not able to adjust his life until after he saw a psychiatrist and understood the role his emotions played in his life, and how they were causing his depression and defeat. It took over a year before he was cured of his depression and was able to keep his weight down as well, but at least he discovered how powerful thoughts can be and how we must keep them under control, instead of letting them control us.

The stories of Cindy P. and Al B. are extreme examples, but I want to impress upon you how important it is for you to get a grip on your willpower to rule your body and be in complete charge of your dieting plan. It's the only way to stay on a straight course and come up a winner by losing.

HYPNOTIZE YOURSELF

If possible, try to solve your emotional problems first before you start your reducing diet. Getting thin first is never the answer. One of the ways you can help your emotions to get under control is to hypnotize yourself. This can be relaxing as well as beneficial to your reducing diet.

1. Sit or lie down.
2. Close your eyes.
3. Think of yourself in a relaxed position, perhaps lying in a hammock watching the leaves of the trees sway in the breeze. When you think you are totally relaxed, and only then, go on to the next step.
4. Slowly count backward from 10 to 1. Picture the numbers being written on a large blackboard. As you say each number, take a deep breath and then slowly let it out. Keep this up until you have counted back to 1. Remain perfectly quiet.
5. At the count of 1, you should be totally relaxed. Now try to imagine a picture of yourself saying no to your favorite food. Next, picture yourself out at a party saying no to food and drink. Visualize yourself passing a bakery window and walking away without a desire to go in and make a selection. Try to flash these pictures onto the back of your mind's eye (your closed eyelids). What you are trying to accomplish is to flash pictures of yourself not giving in to temptation. Perhaps you can think of other situations.

You should try hypnotizing yourself at least twice a day, although you can do this whenever you feel the need. You can also "flash" pictures of the foods you are allowed to eat, thinking about how good they taste.

KEEPING A RECORD

You may find it helpful to make a record of the times when you eat things you shouldn't or when you overeat. List what you ate, how much, who you were with at the time, what room you were in, and the situation. If you see a situation repeating itself with certain conditions, then break away from the habit.

For example, if you find that after a conversation with your mother-in-law on the phone you head for the kitchen for a donut or something sweet, then change your habit to getting a glass of water "because you must be thirsty." Anything to get away from eating. If you find you're always stopping off for an ice cream cone when you pass the local soft ice cream store, change your route so that you won't be tempted in the future.

Learn to substitute a good habit for a bad one. Every time you discover you're eating out of habit instead of because you're actually hungry, do something about it. Then. Right away. Don't wait. You'll be amazed at how much food goes into your stomach without you even realizing it or enjoying it fully.

LEARNING TO ENJOY LIFE MORE

Ask anyone what he wants out of life and he will answer, "Happiness." But ask the question, "What makes you happy?" and you'll get a different answer from everyone. Happiness is an emotion known only to man. Lower animals may experience a type of pleasure, but not happiness. Happiness is such a vague concept that what is happiness to one person is not for another.

To have true happiness, we need to love and be loved as much as we need food to nurture our bodies and a roof over our heads to keep us warm and dry. We merely exist when we have no love in our lives; we don't have happiness. Living has always meant searching for love, even back in the days of the cavemen.

YOUR NEED TO LOVE YOURSELF

When the Lord spoke to Moses and said, "Thou shalt love thy neighbor as thyself" (Leviticus 19:18), he clearly implied the need to love ourselves before we can love others. People who do not like themselves are unable to like or relate to others. Dr. Carl Jung, the famous Swiss psychoanalyst, said, "Acceptance of one's self is the essence of the moral problem and the acid test of one's whole outlook on life."

If you are unhappy, try to find out why. Then, you can either (a) change yourself, or (b) change the situation with which you are living. It is far easier to change yourself. We can't always change jobs, make new friends, move to another city or change the people we have to live with, but we *are* in control of *ourselves* and we *can* make changes in ourselves which will improve life, giving us more happiness and full enjoyment.

Many people confuse self-love with selfishness, but they are really opposites. Selfish people are possessive and demanding. Self-loving people are kind and sharing. Self-loving people know that when you share a pleasure, your own happiness increases. No one who loves himself is out to take all he can and to give as little as possible.

No two of us are exactly alike. We are as different emotionally as we are physically and intellectually, but all of us are faced with the same two problems in our search for happiness:

- The need to do things which please *us* and make *us* happy.
- The need to behave in ways that are acceptable to *other* people.

Yes, we must think about other people around us and what effect we have on their lives. How we treat them will determine how they in turn will treat us. We don't want to be alone. Even in the animal kingdom, very few creatures live solitary lives. We need to feel loved and accepted. If something has been keeping you from enjoying life and being happy, it has probably been you, yourself, and unless you personally do something about it right now, you aren't going to be any happier tomorrow or next week.

CREATE A NEW LIFE FOR YOURSELF

You are already aware that after you lose your excess weight you will be able to enjoy life more, but that doesn't mean you have to wait until that special day arrives. You must *not* wait. You must start right now, this very minute.

Begin by making a list of the hours in your day and how you presently spend them. If you are like most of the women I've talked to about this, you'll discover that you haven't set aside a time of day just for yourself to do something which pleases you, or to do the things which will make you appear more beautiful. How can we learn to relax and enjoy life more if we don't give time to ourselves as well as to the other people in our lives?

Get out of your rut by cultivating a new hobby or interest. Write poetry, paint a picture, learn a new game. Take a course in something you've always been curious about or one which will enable you to better yourself in the job you are doing. Take up a sport such as tennis or handball to help keep you fit.

You have to make time to unlearn the bad habits of a lifetime and replace them with new, good habits that will benefit you as a person instead of dragging you down. As you think about *your* hours and how you will spend them, try to evaluate your life style and what is important to you and to the people you love.

FORGET YOUR AGE

One of the first rules for enjoying life more is never to think about your age. Within reason, you can feel as young as you wish. Have confidence. You have to believe in yourself. If you look at yourself and see a middle-aged spinster or housewife whom life has passed by, that's the way other people are going to think of you, too.

Visualize a woman walking slowly with her shoulders slightly bent, stomach poking out, wearing a disinterested look on her face or even a frown. Won't you think of her as being older, than you would if she stood straight with her head held high, stomach pulled in, and walked with a spring in her step as if she was bursting with energy? If you were going for an acting audition and the director asked you to improvise and show him your impression of an old woman walking across the stage, wouldn't that first description fit perfectly? When you display your body in a youthful way, other people will not think of your age, either. They will accept you for what you are: a vital person, alive with the zest of living.

In this day, one doesn't have to "grow old gracefully." God gave us brains and we can learn all we need to know about beauty aids from reading, practicing and applying those things which are good for us as individuals. A young girl can be excused for not knowing how to make the most of her beauty and inner personality, but not a grown woman who has at her fingertips all the opportunities for learning and doing something about it. What she can't improve with makeup and exercise, she can try to correct with plastic surgery. The woman who is in relatively good health and takes care of her body will always have beauty no matter how old she gets.

There will be times when your shoulders will slump because you are ill or feel depressed, but if you remind yourself how you look this way and how it affects others, you will not only walk with your head held high, but it may also keep you from getting so depressed or feeling so badly.

Try to look good even while doing your household chores. You don't have to wear full makeup, but you can have a dab of lipstick and eye makeup on to lift your spirits, and you should dress in clothes that fit. Who knows who may come to the door and see you in a ratty housecoat and uncombed hair. Don't deliberately put yourself in the position of appearing less than OK.

MAKE YOURSELF FEEL GOOD

Start your day with a shower, but try to have a warm, relaxed evening bath. Pour some fragrant bath oil into your bath while the tub is filling. You might want to try giving yourself a massage while you're waiting (if you don't have someone to do it for you). Self-massage can give you a lot of pleasure as well as relax you.

Either pin your hair up and away from your face or wrap it in a towel. Splash your face with warm water and then wash thoroughly with a washcloth. Rinse with cool water and dry. Using a little baby oil on your fingertips, massage your face, starting with the forehead; then work down the outer sides of the face and over to the chin. Massage around the nose, but not under the eyes. Lastly, massage your neck. Try to use upward strokes all of the time.

As you massage your body, touch yourself in different ways—press, roll and push, but never squeeze too hard. It must never be painful, always pleasurable. Take your time. Don't let anything distract you or interrupt you. Put a note on the door saying that you are taking a nap for an hour and you don't want to be disturbed. Take the phone off the hook. Remember, the purpose is total relaxation and pleasure.

Place your hands at the sides of your neck near the shoulders. Beginning at the shoulders and ending with the base of your head, use your fingertips in a circular movement to massage your neck.

Take your right hand and put it on your left shoulder. Using the fingertips and the palm of the hand, massage the muscles there. Move along to the top of the arm. Now do the other side with the opposite hand.

Massage your back as best you can, reaching back around your waist to get to the opposite side. Squeeze and knead, trying to relax the muscles there as you do. Push and rub, making the movements that seem to feel best for you.

Always be sure to use some baby oil, body lotion or powder when doing your massaging. Don't massage any place where there is inflammation or swelling from an injury. Don't massage any places where you have moles, warts or lumps.

Be extremely gentle as you massage over the chest area, including the breasts. Don't knead, push, squeeze or pinch. Move down to the waist. Squeeze and knead the loose flesh that you find there, doing the same thing as you proceed to the stomach area. Get rougher as you massage your hips and buttocks. Use the whole hand as well as the fingertips to manipulate the fatty area.

Sit down to massage your legs. Place the fingers of both hands on top of your right thigh with the fingers pointing in opposite directions. Knead the flesh with your hands, slowly moving down the leg to your knee. Repeat the motion with the sides and back of the leg. Go to the other leg and do the same.

It may be more comfortable to sit on the floor to do the lower leg. Bring the right knee up so that the sole of the foot is flat on the floor. Use both hands on the sides of your right leg with the fingertips meeting in front over the shinbone. Use the fingertips and the heels of your hands to massage the area. Move your hands around to the back of the leg, massaging and squeezing the calf muscle. Now do the left leg in the same way.

Manipulate your feet with your fingers and the palms of your hands. Squeeze and knead each toe with your fingertips.

Now that you've taken care of your whole body, your fingers may feel a little stiff. Using your left hand, massage your right hand, using just your fingertips. Take the thumb and first finger of your left hand and massage each finger of the right hand in a squeezing, circular motion. Repeat the treatment by alternating hands. Now you're ready for your bath. Soak yourself until the water feels too cool to stay in any longer. Soap your body while standing up and rinse with first a warm and then a cool spray of water. Gently pat your body dry with a large, fluffy towel. For the best quality sleep time, try to get to bed before midnight.

ORGANIZE YOUR LIFE

You can get more out of life if you get your life in better order. Organize your closet and dressing space so you can see what you own. If everything is crammed together, how can you coordinate an outfit quickly? Throw out or give away clothes that you haven't worn for a year or more. Go through your costume jewelry and accessories and evaluate them as to whether you want to keep certain items or not. You have to be able to see what you own or else you forget you have it and it lies unused in a box in a drawer, eventually going out of style. I use little see-through plastic food boxes to separate and store my costume jewelry in a drawer so that when I open the drawer, they are all displayed for easy selection. This also solves the problem of beads becoming tangled.

Read the fashion magazines regularly to keep up with hair-styles, makeup and clothes so that you can interpret and modify them to your own life style. Don't be afraid to try out new cosmetics; you may be missing something that could make you look better.

If you are short, think tall. Remember that many good things come in small packages. Make the most of your petiteness. If you are already tall, reassure yourself that people will look up to you with envy and admiration.

Be feminine and proud that you are a woman. Smile a lot, be enthusiastic about everything you do, be natural, be optimistic, be sincere and be friendly to all.

Good manners are always "in." If you have an argument with someone, keep your voice down and your temper under control.

Try to remember your friends' birthdays, anniversaries or other special days by sending them greeting cards with a personal note.

Never look back. We can't change the past. We can only do something about today and the future. Say to yourself, "Today I am alive. I can enjoy today. Hopefully, if it be God's will, I'll be alive tomorrow and I'll be able to enjoy tomorrow as well." Don't waste precious living time regretting lost youth and opportunities that might have been. Live in the present and plan for the future.

MAKING YOURSELF CHARMING

To enjoy life more, you have to change not only your physical self, but also your inner feelings. Charm is projected from the inside out. All women should try to acquire more charm and the ability to get along well with others. It's never too late to do this. The following ingredients go into my recipe for a charming new you.

Don't talk about your ill health. It's an age giveaway. Don't repeat yourself. That's another sure sign of the aging process. Don't talk about "the good old days." When you bring up the subject of age, you draw attention to it unnecessarily. Eliminate terms such as "you young folks," or "we old people," or "when I was your age."

Make new friends. Go out of your way to help people. Get into the habit of helpfulness. You never know when the person you have helped can be of help to you, although that should not be your motive for treating your fellow man well.

If you want to make friends, you must try to accept others as they are. People don't like to be criticized for what they have done for years. Don't put yourself in the position of being around a person who does something you really dislike, or perhaps you should cut off your relationship with that person completely. You'll never win friends if you are constantly trying to change them.

Don't try to dominate your acquaintances. Nobody likes to be told what to do all the time by another person. It makes him feel that you think he is too stupid to make his own decisions.

Keep your promises. If you tell your neighbor you will pick up a few things from the grocery store for her when you go shopping, write a note to yourself and tape it to your front door so you won't forget. Empty promises are worse than no promises at all.

Try not to show off your possessions or your knowledge. That puts your friends on the defensive and tends to make them feel inferior around you. When they feel this way, they will start to avoid you and look for a friend who is less astute and less successful. You know people who act superior to everyone else and never let you forget how important they think they are. What you have in the way of possessions and brainpower will be evident to others without you having to broadcast it. Try being more subtle.

Try to be honest, and don't exaggerate. Don't be sarcastic. Sometimes you can make a remark in jest if the mood is right, but if it is not quite right, you could say something that sticks in the other person's memory long after you've said it, and builds a growing resentment against you without you being aware of it.

Don't make fun of others' shortcomings. No one likes to be laughed at.

Don't spread gossip. Don't pry into other people's business. Don't laugh too loudly.

Don't pay false compliments. You'll be caught up some day and then nothing you say will be believed no matter how good your intentions.

Don't tell other people what is right and wrong. Don't talk about your personal problems too much even when asked. Change

the subject. Never dominate any conversation. Give the other person
a chance to talk.

Try never to borrow anything.

Keep yourself and your clothing clean.

If you follow some of the rules for charm that I've listed, you
will be well on your way to making people love you more, increasing
your charm and the future pleasures that you will realize because of
it.

4

Common Sense
About Your Nutrition

You must eat well in order to be healthy. Scientists have proven that proper nutrition, provided by good meals, is vital to maintaining health. I don't mean that simply eating well can be a cure-all for preventing or healing all illnesses, but you must realize that when your body is well nourished, it will look better and feel better. If you are overweight, you can eat much less and still provide yourself with proper nutrition.

Many people in the world still suffer from malnutrition as a result of poverty, but many others, even in our country, are improperly nourished not because of poverty, but because of ignorance. Overweight people can be the victims of malnutrition, which can best be described as a deterioration in health resulting from a deficiency or imbalance of nutrients.

STAYING AWAY FROM JUNK FOOD

Even in prosperous North America, we are surrounded by foods that leave us undernourished. Snack foods and "junk foods" of all kinds are loaded with nothing but empty calories, which add to our weight but not to the well-being of our bodies. Misleading advertisements may persuade us that certain worthless foods are good for us. Prime examples are the more popular brands of breakfast cereals for children, sugar-coated and laden with calories, but containing very few actual nutrients.

Many new snacks and foodstuffs appear on the market each year, each one proclaimed as looking great and tasting great and being enriched with vitamins. Have you ever stopped to think, though, why something had to be added to these foods to make them nutritious? They were not actually foods to begin with! Natural foods do not need additives to make them nutritious, but counterfeit foods do.

Why should you settle for less than the best, less than the "real thing"? Put processed and junk foods out of your daily diet and get back to using natural foods. Real foods, natural foods, have all the nutrients in them that your body needs.

My friend Elena was anxious to lose weight very quickly because she was getting married in three months and wanted to wear a size 7 wedding gown instead of a size 10. I told her to try the Amazing 600 Calorie Model's Diet, but to be sure she ate nutritionally balanced meals. She had been eating a lot of junk foods, but made sure during her diet that she stuck to natural foods. Elena was able to achieve her goal in plenty of time to shop for a gown in the smaller size.

THE REAL TROUBLEMAKERS

The biggest culprits in what we eat, the ones that make us overweight in the first place, are carbohydrates. If you are consuming too many carbohydrate foods, you can attribute much of the blame to today's cultural eating patterns. People in our country have grown up with these poor patterns and have passed them on to their children. The main reason too many people eat too many carbohydrate foods is that high carbohydrate foods are the most readily available and seem to be the least expensive.

To include all the nutrients you need for a healthy body, you must learn how to plan your meals. To do this, you should educate yourself about what constitutes a healthy diet. I personally advocate that schools should teach nutrition at all grade levels. Our young people should get proper guidance in what to eat so that they can not only look after their own bodies, but can guard the health and well-being of their own children.

The diet in this book severely limits calories but allows for good nutrition from beginning to end. Whenever your effort to keep your food intake down to 600 calories a day causes you to suspect that you are missing any vital nutrients, be sure that you make up for any losses. Make yourself familiar with all the nutrients your body needs, and be sure that if you miss anything you need on one day, you make up for the missing nutrients on the following day. Never let yourself go for more than a few days without all the elements your body needs to function properly.

There are four main food groups from which you should plan your menus:

- Milk
- Meat, fish, poultry, eggs, peanut butter, dry beans, dry peas and lentils
- Fruits and vegetables
- Breads and cereals

WHY FAD DIETS FAIL

Fad diets that you've heard about or tried yourself all fail because they are not based on a balanced diet. The diet becomes monotonous and boring, and the dieter cannot continue with it. When a diet such as a fad diet consists of only one or a few types of foods, you will not get your necessary nutrients and your body will suffer.

The next thing we have to consider is the makeup of the four food groups so that we can try to make a menu selection that will also give us the vitamins and minerals we need. The three main kinds of foods that your body uses for energy and building and replacing cells are protein, fats and carbohydrates.

Proteins are known as the tissue builders and they contain carbon, hydrogen, oxygen, nitrogen and sometimes sulphur. Next to water, the body contains more protein than any other component. The complex molecules in protein are made up of amino acids. When we put amino acids into our stomachs, chemicals there react to them and the end result may be one of several possibilities:

• They may be used to create body proteins.

• They may be oxidized for immediate energy.

• They may be converted to carbohydrates.

• They may be transformed into fat.

• They may be excreted by the body.

It's no wonder why proteins are so important to your body's well-being. Too little protein retards growth and causes malnutrition. Too much protein overworks the liver and kidneys, but it is doubtful that you will ever be in danger of eating too much protein, the main reason being that it is contained in the most expensive foods. Foods containing the highest protein value are meat, dairy products, fish and soybeans.

Fats are the energy reservoirs and should be used sparingly by the obese person and in moderation by the average person. Fats contain carbon, hydrogen and oxygen. The hardness or softness of fats and their melting points are determined by the particular fatty acids they contain. The lower the number of carbon atoms in the fatty acid, the softer the fat. The lower the melting point of a fat, the more readily it will be digested. The hard fats that are found in gravies, sauces, fried foods, rich desserts and fat meat retard digestion. Olive, corn, cottonseed and peanut oils are compounds containing oleic acid, so they are softer, unsaturated fats. Besides furnishing fuel for the body, fats are the carriers of the fat soluble vitamins A, D, K and E, which we need for the health of our hair, skin and all epithelial tissue. Because fats slow down the digestive process and the emptying of the stomach, we tend to feel full for a longer time than we would after eating other kinds of food. About a fourth of the day's calories should be obtained from fat. Too much fat in the diet will give you feelings of nausea, aside from making you overweight.

Carbohydrates include sugars, starches and cellulose, and are made up of carbon, hydrogen and oxygen. The burning of the carbon from the starch or sugar produces heat or energy. About 60 percent of the day's total calories should be provided by carbohydrates for the efficient production of energy. The chief fuel in your body is the simple sugar, glucose. Without glucose, your nervous system would not function, your muscles wouldn't move and your brain couldn't think. Fortunately, carbohydrate foods are the cheapest foods to buy and the easiest to obtain.

THE ROLE OF VITAMINS

Each *vitamin* has a definite purpose in helping your body to operate efficiently. Vitamin A promotes growth and is essential for the chemical processes of vision. A deficiency in vitamin A can cause poor vision in dim light or even result in night blindness. It is also essential for reproduction, lactation, the proper formation of tooth enamel and for the health of the epithelial tissues. The principal source of vitamin A in the diet is likely to be plant foods which have high green or yellow colorings. There is a direct relationship between the greenness of a leaf and its carotene content. Dark green leaves are rich in carotene, but the pale leaves of lettuce and cabbage are insignificant sources. The best sources of vitamin A are spinach, turnip tops, chard, beet greens, parsley, bell peppers, asparagus and broccoli. Yellow vegetables include carrots, sweet potatoes, winter squash and pumpkin. Yellow fruits containing vitamin A are apricots, peaches, papaya and cantaloupe. Fish liver oils contain vitamin A, as do milk, butter, fortified margarines, whole-milk cheese, liver and egg yolk. Vitamin A is not lost by the usual cooking temperatures, but the wilting or dehydration of foods may result in considerable losses. Canned and frozen foods retain their maximal values for about a year.

The B vitamins are most effective when taken together in your diet. Vitamin B_1, also known as thiamin, was the first of the B-complex vitamins to be discovered. A lack of vitamin B_1 can make you tired, irritable and unable to concentrate. Abnormal heart rhythm, lifeless hair, constipation and distension of the abdomen can also occur if the B_1 intake is too low. Thiamin can be found in wheat germ, yeast, bran, lean pork, nuts, heart, liver, whole grain breads and cereals. Vitamin B_2 (riboflavin) is necessary for the proper functioning of the gastro-intestinal tract, the health of the cutaneous system and the visual apparatus. It is also needed for the formation of the blood, to promote growth in all age groups, for longer life and the better weaning of infants. When there is a deficiency of vitamin B_2 in your diet, you will age earlier, have a lowered resistance to infection, lose your hair and have visual difficulties. The best food sources for B_2 are yeast, liver, kidney, heart, wheat germ, cheddar cheese, eggs, leafy vegetables and nuts.

Niacin was once thought to be the same as B_1 and later it appeared to be the same as B_2, but it is neither. Niacin is necessary for the oxidation of carbohydrates, for proper functioning of the digestive tract, for the normal tissue metabolism of the body and for growth. A lack of it could result in the disease called pellagra. The best sources of this vitamin are glandular tissues, lean meats, salmon, whole cereals, seeds, legumes and nuts.

Pyridoxine, or vitamin B_6 helps in the utilization of unsaturated fatty acids and the metabolism of amino acids. A deficiency of this vitamin may result in irritability, insomnia and nervousness. Whole cereals, peanut oil, eggs, molasses, nuts, legumes, meats and milk are good sources.

Vitamin B_{12} promotes growth and is necessary for the maturing of the red blood cells. It is found in liver, kidneys and meat.

There are also some lesser known B vitamins. Choline and inositol have been found to play a role in preventing and relieving hardening of the arteries. The foods that are highest in inositol are wheat germ, oranges, grapefruit, watermelon, green peas, lean beef heart, dry peas and beef brains. Choline also protects the liver and kidneys. Foods rich in choline are beef liver, spinach, string beans, cooked cabbage, lamb kidney, egg yolk and wheat germ. Biotin is made in appreciable amounts in the intestinal tract and for that reason one is less likely to be deficient in this B vitamin than any other. Beef liver is the food containing the most biotin. Pantothenic acid is the B vitamin which stabilizes the adrenal glands and is thought to help keep the natural color of the hair. Again, beef liver is the best source. Folic acid is an important B vitamin, essential to the proper formation of red blood and also to the growth of the cells. A large quantity is not needed but is found most frequently in salmon, watermelon, oysters, spinach and dry cooked lima beans.

Vitamin C (ascorbic acid) is essential for the health of the gums, development of the teeth and the metabolism of carbohydrates, fats and proteins. It promotes the healing of mucous tissue and stimulates the production of bone marrow and cortical hormones. It cannot be stored in the body and since it is water soluble, all of the day's quota should not be taken at one time. If you do not use all of the vitamin C you put into your body within 3 hours, it will be excreted. The best sources are all kinds of citrus fruits, raw vegetables and liver.

Vitamin D can be found only in a few foods in significant amounts, and it can be absorbed into the blood only in the presence of fat. It prevents the loss of calcium from the bones and the teeth during pregnancy, expedites the utilization of phosphorus by the

bones and increases cell metabolism and the retention of phos-
phatase in the bones. If you get enough sunshine, vitamin D is
produced in the skin through the exposure of the body to it. Some
types of fish, fish liver oils and egg yolks contain vitamin D.

Vitamin E was discovered in 1922. It preserves vitamin A and
prevents the oxidation and off-flavors in foods which contain fat. It
is essential for the prevention of sterility in males and miscarriages
in females. Good sources are cereal, vegetables, milk, meats, leaves
of plants and vegetable oils.

Vitamin F is commonly known as essential fatty acids. All of
the golden vegetable oils such as vegetable, wheat germ, linseed,
sunflower, safflower and soybean oils are the best sources.

Vitamin K is essential for the formation of prothrombin, an
enzyme which is necessary for the clotting of blood. It can be found
in alfalfa, leafy vegetables, cauliflower, tomatoes, kale, liver,
soybean oils, pork fat, egg yolk and milk.

THE ROLE OF MINERALS

Besides vitamins, your body also needs *minerals*. They help to
maintain the amount of water in the body that is necessary for life
processes. They keep blood and tissue from becoming too acid or
too alkaline. They influence the secretion of glands and help to draw
chemical substances into and out of the cells. They help to set up
conditions responsible for the irritability and contractibility of
muscle and tissue and are important in sending messages through the
nervous system. It is believed that the mineral elements required for
a healthy body are calcium, phosphorus, potassium, iron, iodine,
copper, sulphur, sodium, magnesium, manganese, cobalt, zinc and
traces of others. Because all minerals are water soluble, the water in
which foods are cooked has nutritional value.

Calcium is found in milk, cheese and the stems and leaves of
plants. The calcium of spinach, chard and beet greens is not as
readily absorbed as is that found in broccoli, kale and cauliflower.
Calcium is needed for coagulation of the blood, construction of teeth
and bones, muscular contraction, tone, osmosis, growth and assim-
ilation of iron from the intestinal tract.

Phosphorus is found in meat, eggs, cheese, fish, milk and the
parts of plants which reproduce, such as seeds and cereals. The

metabolism of carbohydrates cannot take place without phosphorus. It is also needed to harden and give rigidity to the teeth and bones.

Iron is essential for hemoglobin formation, growth, the oxidation of food, all secretions of the tissues and reproduction. The best sources of iron are eggs, liver, peanuts, peas, carrots, celery, apples, apricots, bananas, cherries, peaches and molasses. Lesser amounts are found in potatoes, figs, grapefruit, pineapple, whole cereals and legumes.

Copper plays a part in the transformation of iron into hemoglobin. It is stored in the liver and is also needed for the pigmentation of the skin and hair. All livers are excellent sources of copper. Other good sources are chocolate, cocoa, molasses, whole cereals, apricots, Brazil nuts, pecans, mushrooms and walnuts.

Iodine is needed for metabolism and the activity of the thyroid gland. It is also necessary for normal growth and height. Most fruits and vegetables grown where the iodine content of the water and soil is adequate will contain an ample supply of iodine. When in doubt, use iodized salt.

Potassium and magnesium act as a balance to sodium chloride. Vegetables, meats and cereals are good sources of these minerals. Sulphur is needed for growth, the health of the skin, hair and nails, and for the treatment of all infections. Sulphur is found in protein foods and in some vegetables. Although we need only 3 grams of salt a day, most people use about 10. It increases the metabolism of proteins, acts as an aid to carbohydrate metabolism and regulates the osmotic pressure of the body fluids. Too much salt in the diet will enlarge the kidneys.

Zinc is present in the thyroid and sex glands. It is one of the constituents of insulin, which is necessary for the normal utilization of sugar. Liver and milk are good sources.

Cobalt is also found in small amounts in most of the organs of the human body. It appears to be related to the development of red corpuscles. In persistent anemia, doctors may recommend cobalt, iron and copper. Liver of all kinds is the best source of cobalt, iron and copper.

Manganese is found in green leaves and whole grain breads and cereals, but its exact function in the body is not yet understood.

There are over 20 amino acids, but only eight of them are essential for health and a longer life. The rest can be manufactured in the body. For this reason, it is very important to eat large amounts of first-class protein foods which contain the essential eight, such as milk, lean meats, eggs, yeast and soybeans.

A former model named Jennifer had begun neglecting herself. One day she gasped when she looked down at her bathroom scale and saw that it registered 150 pounds. Jennifer had never been that heavy in her life. At her height of 5′ 6″ she should have weighed no more than about 125 pounds. She came to me and pleaded with me to help her lose weight fast. I explained that there was no really fast, safe way to lose 25 pounds, and that she would have to become a dedicated dieter for several months if she wanted my help.

Jennifer agreed to follow my model's diet, and she learned something about vitamins and nutrition while she did. She ate more balanced meals, but she stuck to the diet, and lost 5 pounds the first week.

She was very pleased, but during the second week she only lost 2 pounds, and the following week only 3. The fourth week Jennifer didn't lose any weight at all because she was getting tired of dieting and forgot to keep a record of how much she was eating. I explained the importance of following a careful plan all over again.

During her fifth week, Jennifer followed the diet strictly, but only lost 1 pound. She refused to be discouraged and, during the following seven weeks, Jennifer lost on the average of 2 pounds a week. Although it took Jennifer three months to lose her 25 excess pounds, she thinks the diet is truly amazing, because her weight has stayed down at the lower level that is more suitable for her height. Jennifer feels that she is better prepared to keep her weight down now that she knows about nutrition and counting calories.

With the knowledge you have gained from this chapter, you too will now be able to plan your menus, limiting yourself to 600 calories per day, and still keep your health. Use my menu selections at first to get you well acquainted with the plan and then you'll be able to use your creative ability to make your meals appealing to your own personal tastes.

5

How to Use Fasting
As Part of Your Diet

Some of you will find fasting to be a helpful part of your diet. Fasting means giving up all food and drink, with the exception of water, for a chosen length of time. It has been called the ultimate diet, because if you eat nothing at all, you are 100 percent sure of losing weight. Even so, I don't want you to think of a fast as a means of losing weight, but only, if you choose, as a kind of catalyst for your total weight reduction regimen.

Most people can safely fast for one to three days. Longer fasts, however, are likely to be dangerous. Before starting any fast, even if you believe you are in perfect health, check with your doctor to make sure. Find out if there is any health problem you may have that could make it dangerous for you to go without food for one to three days.

There are certain persons who should never fast, such as children, pregnant women, women who have just given birth and many elderly people. Some older people can fast without harm, but again, it is best to get the blessing of your doctor first. If you have any of the following physical conditions, you should not try a fast: heart disease, bleeding ulcers, cancer, gout, tumors, blood disease, active pulmonary disease, juvenile diabetes, kidney disease, liver disease, cerebral disease or recent myocardial infarction.

And if you try fasting, don't let failure discourage you. Don't feel that your dieting is a failure if you can only make it through one day of a fast that you had planned to last for three days. It's not the length of the fast that we're interested in, just the breaking of a poor eating habit, and for that purpose one day can suffice as well as three.

FASTING IS NOT STARVATION

During a fast, you do not eat any food or drink any beverage which has calories. A pure fast allows only water, with distilled water being the preference over any other kind. Going on a short fast is not starving yourself, as you may tend to think, for starving can only occur when the body uses up its stored resources. When you start your fast, your body will nourish itself from the nutritive matter it already contains so that your system will continue to function normally. In doing this, you will automatically start to lose weight in dramatic amounts, which will give you an incentive to stick with your 600 calorie diet plan for as long as you need it.

FASTING IS AS OLD AS MANKIND

There are over 70 references to fasting in the Old and New Testaments. The Pharisees held the fast in high esteem, but paid more attention to its strict observance than to the spirit with which they carried it out. Jesus fasted for 40 days in the desert before beginning his public ministry. He was especially critical of the Pharisees, for he felt that they were not using their fasting practices for humility or godliness. Many Christians fast during Lent, the period of 40 days from Ash Wednesday until Easter, commemorating the fast of Jesus, but this is usually only a token fast of abstaining from certain foods or drink. Jewish law orders a yearly fast on the Day of Atonement, known as Yom Kippur. Many Orthodox Jews follow the custom in which the bride and groom fast on the day before the wedding. During Ramadan, the ninth month of the Moslem year, Moslems fast. This fasting takes place from sunrise until sunset every day. Buddhists and Hindus also use fasting in their religious practices. In early religions, fasting was used to keep the gods happy and to improve the food supply. Many people have used the fast to obtain forgiveness for their misdeeds. In some religions, it has been used at times of mourning. For others, fasting has been a way of finding spiritual joy.

FASTING HAS BEEN USED FOR MANY PURPOSES

Early Egyptians believed that by fasting for three days a month, you could preserve good health and happiness. Pythagoras, the Greek mathematician, believed that fasting made the mental processes more alert, and he would fast for 40 days and urge his students to do the same. Plutarch once said it was better to go on a fast than to take medicine. Syrians, Mongolians and Druid priests also practiced fasting.

In the tenth and eleventh centuries, Arab physicians prescribed three-week fasts to cure syphilis and smallpox. In the seventeenth and eighteenth centuries, the English and German people discovered that fasting was beneficial in treating illness. Russians came to a similar conclusion in the eighteenth and nineteenth centuries. Fasting was used in hospitals in Napoleon's time as a treatment for venereal disease. Fasting was observed in the colonial days of our country just as strictly as the Puritan Sabbath. North American Indians used fasting to give themselves endurance and strength.

Sometimes fasting is used as a means of public protest or to further political goals. Mohandas Gandhi of India is a prime example, as is comedian Dick Gregory. Yogis fast with the hope of embracing a new mysticism. It's a fact that fasting can give you a "high" feeling. At first it is a restful, calming experience that relieves anxieties and then progresses to a feeling of true exhilaration. It is no wonder that it is proclaimed as the means to produce spiritual consciousness.

YOUR MIND MUST RULE YOUR BODY
IF YOU ARE TO DIET SUCCESSFULLY

Fasting not only brings a rest to your digestive system, but also to your central nervous system. We must begin thinking and believing that we must eat to live and not live to eat. Food can be a blessing or a curse, but we must be the masters and control our eating habits. We have been literally trained to think that we must have food by the clock whether we are actually hungry or not. We have become slaves to food, eating and drinking at certain times of the day just because everyone else is doing it. Our social life demands it. In addition to overeating, we also have the cocktail hour which eventually can lead to alcohol addiction, robbing our bodies of vitality and good health. In Chapter 10, we'll deal with the social aspects of dieting. The body can take a lot of abuse from overfeeding, but eventually this causes weakness and makes us more susceptible to diseases of every nature. We would all be much healthier if we didn't eat so much food. When you start this diet, you will be amazed at how little food it takes to nourish your body and keep it functioning in good order. The best way to gain control over your eating habits (or, should I say, your overeating habits) is to begin with a fast. It helps you lose the memory of enjoying food as a pastime, so you don't miss it as much when you actually start your diet. It gives you a feeling that your stomach is smaller and doesn't need as much food to fill it. A successful fast puts you in charge of your body again, so that you can control yourself and adhere to a weight reducing program. While you are on your fast, you will lose weight faster than at any other time in your diet, so it will give you an incentive to go a step further. Fasting to lose weight has not been popular only because food plays such an important role in our lives. Take away the importance of food as a source of "entertainment," and use food only as a fuel for the furnace to keep your body going, and you will no longer worship food.

FASTING IS A THERAPEUTIC MEANS OF REGAINING YOUR HEALTH

Have you ever noticed at times when you were sick that you lost your appetite and didn't feel like eating any food at all? This was your natural instinct setting off an alarm in your brain, telling you to fast to help your body heal itself. A fast will get rid of poisons which have accumulated inside you and which drain you of your energy and good health. That's why sick or wounded animals refuse to eat. Their instinct of self-preservation takes away their hunger and they fast, knowing that it will eventually help them to feel better.

It is almost impossible these days to buy food that is completely free from insect sprays and synthetic food additives, and this is why our systems are so clogged with poisons. We must do everything we can to eliminate these toxins, which otherwise will become cumulative and destroy our vigor. Very few of us are in a position to grow all of the food we eat in order to control the end result, so we have to find other means to cleanse our systems. Fasting is the easiest and most natural way to do this. Whenever possible, try to eat organically grown foods—those which are close to nature—and keep away from all chemically preserved foods. Some of the things which have been poisoning your body in the past include: coffee, tea, alcoholic beverages, tobacco, smoked fish, lunch meats (such as hot dogs, salami, bologna, corned beef, pastrami and any meats which contain sodium nitrate or nitrite), dried fruits containing sulphur dioxide and chickens which have been injected with stilbestrol or fed with chicken feed that contains drugs. When buying canned soups, look at the label and watch out for benzoate of soda and salted foods such as nuts, pretzels, potato chips, salted crackers and sauerkraut.

FASTING AWAKENS THE MIND

Each time you fast, you will notice that your mind seems to grow sharper and more positive. The Greek philosopher Socrates and his disciple Plato believed that fasting helped the brain achieve the ultimate efficiency, so they advocated ten-day fasts. I enjoy fasting because my senses become more alert to everything around me. It's a joy to be able to discern the various fragrances making up the air I breathe, instead of experiencing only one aroma. The first thing I notice about a fast is that a kind of calm comes over me, but at the same time I feel better able to think and work out any problems which come up during my day.

Recently, while I was doing some research at the university library, I overheard Sherry H., a college student, talking to a friend. It seemed she was becoming so uptight about preparing her term paper that she was not able to work on it properly. She found every excuse to put off doing it, and yet her deadline was drawing near and she knew she'd have to start soon. Otherwise, she would not get it done and might get a failing grade as a result. I couldn't help but suggest to her that she try a fast of one to three days. Instead of taking offense at my overhearing her predicament and offering my unasked for advice, she seemed elated that there might be a solution to the problem and listened intently while I explained some facts about fasting and what could be accomplished with it. I noticed while I was talking with her that she could have stood to lose 5 or 10 pounds, but I made no mention of it. Several weeks later I ran into her again at the library and she told me how she had tried the fast for two days while she worked on her term paper. She claimed that it made her think more clearly, and she became disciplined enough to complete her assignment without anxiety. She thanked me for suggesting it and told me how, as a side effect, she had lost 5 pounds and now had the willpower to stay on a reducing diet to lose 5 more.

Fasting has been used as therapy to help the mentally ill. In cases where regular therapy had failed to help certain patients whose lives had deteriorated so badly that they were not functioning normally and were uneasy about the future, fasting was tried as a last resort. After fasting, many were able to resume their lives with renewed confidence in living. In experiments with schizophrenics in Russia, Canada and the United States, it was found that 70 percent showed a marked improvement.

WATER IS YOUR BEST FRIEND DURING A FAST

During your fast, it is important that you drink large amounts of water, preferably distilled water. Distilled water is pure water, a compound of two parts hydrogen and one part oxygen. If you don't have distilled water from a bottle, you can collect rain water or melted snow, which is pure water since it has been distilled by nature. We can live for a long time without any food, but our bodies cannot survive for very long without water. If you are used to drinking coffee, tea, beer, wine or stronger alcoholic drinks, you should give them up during your fast and only use water.

The purpose of the fast is not only to shrink your appetite but also to cleanse your body by flushing out all of the many poisons which may be buried within it. By drinking lots of water, this is accomplished quicker and more easily, and it keeps you from becoming dangerously dehydrated.

Marilyn R. was an acquaintance of mine whose weight problem got worse with the birth of each of her children. She had tried all of the fad diets she came across in the women's magazines that she read, but she never could stay on any one of them long enough to lose more than 3 or 4 pounds before she started to gain back what she had lost. As she was telling me about this one day, I asked her if she had ever tried fasting. She said, "Oh, you mean just drink fruit juices for several days instead of eating food? I've tried that, too, but I can't stand to drink liquids all day long. I have to have solid food." Then I had to explain to her that what she was talking about was a juice fast and not a true fast. I went on to tell her that it was easier to give up food entirely for a few days than to just drink liquids such as fruit juices, which have a lot of carbohydrates and stimulate your hunger. She was able to use her willpower for long enough to stay on a three-day fast and then start my Amazing 600 Calorie Model's Diet. By doing this, she lost 10 pounds in 10 days and is well on her way at this time to reaching her goal of 115 pounds, which is about right for her 5'4" height.

HOW LONG SHOULD YOU FAST?

How long you should fast depends on you and how you feel as you fast. It also depends on how long your doctor believes you can fast safely, since he knows more about your physical health than you do. There is no need to go on a fast for longer than one to three days in order to ready yourself for starting the Amazing 600 Calorie Model's Diet. We are not interested in breaking any fasting records. We are only trying to change or modify your eating habits and even a one-day fast can help you do that. Longer fasts should only be undertaken with the constant strict supervision of a physician. If you like the idea of fasting and can carry it out easily, you could form a habit of fasting for one day a week, which would help you to lose weight that much faster. You could start out with a one-day fast for the first week and then the next week fast for two days, thereby building up your willpower and your ability to stand the effects of fasting. Most experts extol fasting only as a method of cleansing the body for better health and not as an aid to weight reduction. Even the experts disagree on how long you should fast to get the best results.

There are fasting resorts in England where they feel that the 30-day fast is best. At German fasting resorts they believe that the ideal fast is 21 days. The French say 14 days is ideal. There are also fasting resorts in the United States where fasting is medically supervised for periods of up to 30 days.

STARTING YOUR FAST

As you start your fast, you'll experience a craving for food, but this is not actually hunger. Be sure to keep telling yourself this. Your body is accustomed to being fed at certain times of the day and this is just a natural reflex from those old habits.

The best time of day to start your fast is in the morning, because you have already been without food since your evening meal the day before. To take the place of tea or coffee, drink hot water (during the winter) or ice water (during the summer). You won't believe me until you try it yourself, but hot water is really quite palatable. Most health faddists will tell you not to drink ice water, but if the weather is very warm it will help you with your fast a lot better than lukewarm water from the tap, which can be a lot less appetizing. Drink water whenever you feel hungry. Simply tell yourself, "I'm not really hungry, I'm only thirsty." Sip your water slowly, like you might a fine wine. Don't gulp it down in large amounts. Keep busy for all of your waking hours. Don't put yourself in the position of searching for something to eat just because you have nothing better to do with your time. Play some old records, clean out a closet or mend some clothes. Do anything to take your mind off eating, especially during those times when you have been conditioned to look forward to eating, such as breakfast, lunch and dinner. Don't watch the food commercials on TV. Turn them off or leave the room. Go to another room or leave the house when others are having their meals. As you drink your water, think to yourself: "This water is purifying my body, washing out all the collected poisons there. The more I drink, the cleaner I'll be." Try to get as much sleep as possible and don't plan any strenuous activities.

On about the third day of the fast, you will lose the feeling of hunger and many people want to go on fasting for a longer time because of this. At this time, you start breathing more easily and you lose any feeling of fatigue you may have experienced at the beginning.

GLORIA'S TWO DISCOVERIES

Gloria knew she was 40 pounds overweight. She hated going places anymore because her clothes didn't fit her properly, and when she went shopping to find ones that did, she discovered that there wasn't much of a selection in the larger sizes. Everything looked too matronly and Gloria was only 27 and didn't feel any older than that. One day, however, Gloria confronted herself in the mirror and discovered the truth. She had to go on a diet immediately because she refused to look older than she was. She had a feeling that she actually looked older than her husband, who was seven years her senior. She began to wonder how he had put up with her during the past few years since she had gained so much weight. She hoped he would forgive her past overindulgences and give her the encouragement she needed to stay on the diet plan for the length of time she needed in order to lose 40 pounds. He was overjoyed when she told him about her plan. She began her diet with a short fast and it took only nine weeks for her to go from 177 pounds down to 137 pounds which was just right for her 5'7" frame. She lost weight at the rate of 4½ pounds per week. Gloria has discovered how much more fun life can be. She's learned from her past mistakes and vows she'll never be fat again. I believe her, too!

Bernarr Macfadden, who was the founder of the physical culture movement in the United States, said, "It is not the number of years you live on this earth, it is how you have lived. Regardless of age, Mother Nature will give you the opportunity to make a complete comeback." You too can begin a new life, so start thinking and believing that, with the start of your fast, you are starting anew. Refuse to grow old by doing everything you can to keep your body looking young and functioning well. The first step toward that goal is to burn up all the extra food you consume. Put that energy to better use. Fast and be fit!

6

Starting Your
Amazing 600 Calorie
Model's Diet

The best time to start your diet is when you can give top priority to losing weight. There is no perfect time for everyone. Some times are better than others, but only you can make the choice of when you think is best for you.

It's best to start a diet just as soon as you make up your mind that this time you will follow the rules and lose weight successfully. Never start a diet when you are under any kind of emotional strain. The wrong time to start would be if you are moving, starting college, looking for a job or facing a crisis in the family. Situations like this demand a lot of your strength, both physical and emotional. Food becomes overly important to you in times of stress and you may find yourself using food as a tranquilizer instead of as fuel for your body.

Once you find what you think is the right time to start, don't procrastinate. It's too easy to make weak excuses and put things off.

TAKE TEMPTATION AWAY

Try to keep foods that you must not eat out of your line of vision. Don't keep dishes of candy or nuts in the living room. Put the crackers and snacks that the rest of the family eats in another part of the closet that you will never open. Hide the pudding dishes behind the can of grapefruit juice in the refrigerator. Cover leftovers with aluminum foil or opaque plastic covers so they will be out of sight. Spend as little time as you can in the kitchen for that's where temptation lives. Don't wander into the kitchen even for a drink of water; you can always get that in the bathroom. When you're out, avoid driving past the ice cream store or bakery. Whatever you do, don't walk past a bakery and look in. When stopping at the supermarket, always use a list and avoid the bakery and junk food sections.

DISCOVER YOUR WEAKNESSES

You know you are overweight because you have eaten too much food in the past, but let's find out why you overeat. *Why* do you eat too much, *what* do you eat too much of, and *when* do you do all this overeating? You may not be able to answer this without going to the trouble of keeping a record of everything you eat for at least one week before you start your diet. This is the best way to find out the answers. It's embarrassing to put down that you ate a dozen cookies at one sitting, but embarrassing or not, put down everything that you eat or drink in a little notebook you can carry with you. Carry your calorie counter as well so you can note the calorie count at the same time. If you don't do it then, it will be harder for you to get caught up later on.

You must write *everything* down, every potato chip, every nut, everything that goes into your mouth. Try to eat normally, as you usually do. You should start your diet after you have kept a record for one week. This record-keeping will educate you about yourself. You'll discover some interesting things about your eating patterns.

Ellen V. suddenly found herself 20 pounds above her ideal weight. She couldn't understand how this had happened. After keeping records of everything she ate, and when, during the course of a week, Ellen discovered that she always ate something sweet, like a piece of Danish pastry or several cookies, right after she talked with her husband on the phone. Her husband didn't realize it, but when he asked Ellen what she had been doing all day, he was putting her on the defensive. He was only making conversation, but Ellen took it as a criticism that maybe she wasn't doing as much as she should be doing. She usually had so little to report that she was made to feel guilty by the question. To overcome her guilty feelings, to relieve her distress, she ate something sweet, and since eating something made her feel better, it got to be a daily habit.

Once she looked at her own record, though, Ellen became aware that this was the chief cause of her extra weight. She acknowledged her own feelings, and was no longer troubled by a guilty conscience, even when she had to report to her husband that she had done nothing of any importance that day.

At the same time, she put herself on my Amazing 600 Calorie Model's Diet and followed it carefully. Within three weeks, while enjoying three full meals every day, Ellen V. got rid of her 20 excess pounds.

The best way to keep a record of your own eating habits is to write down everything on a small, handy pad such as a steno pad. At the top of the page, put the date and how much you weigh that day. Always weigh yourself at the same time each morning, preferably without your clothes.

Every time you eat or drink something, write it in a column down the center of the page. To the left of the column, write in the time of day when you ate that food or drank that beverage. Buy yourself a scale to weigh your food. Try to make note of the correct portion. If you haven't been doing it each day, then at the end of the week look up the calorie counts of all the foods you ate and put these figures in the column to the right, adding up each day's worth of calories. Try not to feel guilty about eating at this particular time. Just eat what you feel like eating. You have to remember that you will be going on a strict diet next week, so eat the hot fudge sundae or chocolate eclair now, since you won't be doing it again for a long time. Indulge yourself and get it out of your system. Don't worry that you might put on more weight. It's really unlikely. You've been putting off going on a diet for so long now that one more week isn't going to make a difference. Tell yourself that this is an experiment; you're going to find out what makes you tick.

The first thing you will find out by doing this little experiment is that you are eating more calories than you thought you were. You will also find that you have an eating pattern, certain times of the day when you are under stress and may eat more than at other times.

How we cope with stress varies from individual to individual. Some people will eat sweets, some will stuff themselves with snack food and others will drink alcohol—all laden with many calories. When I'm feeling down and depressed, nothing makes me feel better than a glass of milk and some cookies. A psychologist would probably claim this to be a holdover from my childhood days when my mother would give me milk and cookies if I hurt myself or as a reward for doing something well. There's no doubt about it. I know that milk and cookies have caused me to put on weight and I am very careful now to eat no more than two cookies at a time. So you can see why keeping these records can help you, too.

Please try to be as honest as possible about keeping these records. No one else will see them and it will tell you so much about yourself. When your week is over, use a calorie counter and figure out what your total was for every day. Now figure out your average for each day. This is your maintenance calorie count for the weight you are at right now. You will have to eat less than that amount to lose weight. You can figure out how much less by subtracting 600 calories from that figure.

THE FIRST WEEK OF YOUR DIET

THE FIRST DAY

You should fast from food completely on the first day of your diet. That means nothing with calories in it, not even juices. (If your doctor advises you not to fast, you should eat as little as he permits.) You may have all you want of the following: water, no-calorie sodas, black coffee and tea.

Try to keep busy all day doing something, anything to keep your mind from wandering and thinking about food and eating. This is a good time to clean out the garage, straighten up a closet or start a new hobby.

There are two good reasons for fasting for one or more days at the start of your diet:

- You show an immediate weight loss the next day which bolsters your spirits and your willpower for continuing your diet.

- It helps break the eating pattern which has led you to become overweight. When you resume eating, it is easier to control your appetite.

THE SECOND DAY

Breakfast

53	½ grapefruit
77	1 soft cooked egg
60	1 slice cracked wheat bread
190	Total calories

Lunch

100	½ can beef soup diluted with water
50	5 wheat or rye thins (crackers)
35	1 fresh peach or ½ canned peach
185	Total calories

Dinner

117	3 ounces broiled chicken, skin removed
33	1 fresh (average 2½" diameter) tomato
22	½ cup boiled or canned spinach
27	3 pecan halves, chopped (sprinkle on spinach)
199	Total calories

Total calories for the day: 574

THE THIRD DAY

Breakfast

43	1 cup puffed wheat cereal
45	4 ounces skim milk
87	1 average banana, (6¾" long)
175	Total calories

Lunch

64	5 boiled shrimp
75	3 tablespoons cocktail sauce
6	3 average lettuce leaves (iceberg)
54	3 Ritz crackers
199	Total calories

Dinner

160 4 ounces ocean perch, broiled with 2 teaspoons butter
33 1 fresh (average 2½" diameter) tomato
22 ½ cup green beans
 11 1 saltine cracker
226 Total calories

Total calories for the day: 600

THE FOURTH DAY

Breakfast

56 1 cup fresh strawberries
 89 8 ounces skim milk
145 Total calories

Lunch

72 2 ounces tuna (water packed)
78 ¾ oz. domestic Swiss cheese
 8 ¼ fresh cucumber
 7 ½ fresh green pepper
17 ½ fresh tomato (2½" diameter)
 6 3 lettuce leaves (iceberg)
81 1 tablespoon blue cheese dressing (on top of salad mixture
      of above ingredients)
269 Total calories

Dinner

78 1 slice bologna
88 1 cup tomato soup (diluted with ½ can water)
20 1 double square Rye-Krisp (Put the bologna between the
      Rye-Krisp)
186 Total calories

Total calories for the day: 600

THE FIFTH DAY

Breakfast

58 ½ fresh cantaloupe
 60 ¼ cup cottage cheese
118 Total calories

Lunch

154 2 hard cooked eggs
 17 ½ fresh tomato (2½" diameter)
 24 4 Cheez-it crackers
195 Total calories

Dinner

117 3 ounces broiled chicken, skin removed
  2 1 lettuce leaf (iceberg)
  8 ¼ fresh cucumber (about 7" long)
 17 ½ fresh tomato (2½" diameter)
  4 ¼ green pepper (mix with lettuce, cucumber and tomato into a salad)
 71 1 ear corn (about 5" long), boiled
 61 1 navel orange (about 3" diameter)
280 Total calories

Total calories for the day: 593

THE SIXTH DAY

Breakfast

154 2 eggs scrambled in a Teflon pan
 35 1 slice Gluten bread
 36 2 teaspoons jelly
225 Total calories

Lunch

 87 1 average banana (6¾" long)
 89 8 ounces skim milk
176 Total calories

Dinner

112 2 ounces baked flounder
 30 ½ cup chopped broccoli (frozen)
 23 ½ cup cooked carrots
 34 5 almonds cut up and sprinkled over the fish
199 Total calories

Total calories for the day: 600

THE SEVENTH DAY

Breakfast

53 ½ grapefruit
77 1 soft cooked egg
 74 1 slice pumpernickel bread
204 Total calories

Lunch

65 ½ can chicken noodle soup (diluted with water)
89 8 ounces skim milk flavored with 1 teaspoon vanilla and
___ sweetened with any no-cal sweetener
154 Total calories

Dinner

189 3 ounces chuck roast
23 ½ cup cooked carrots
 30 ½ small boiled potato
242 Total calories

Total calories for the day: 600

The menus provided in this chapter, as well as the menus in Chapter 7, are only suggestions and do not have to be followed unless they appeal to your appetite. Use the information in the calorie counter section of the book to put together menus according to your particular tastes. Just keep in mind that your total calorie count for the day must be no more than 600 calories.

7

Sample Menus for Meals of Only 600 Calories a Day

My friend Yvonne didn't like the idea of counting calories day after day, but she knew she had to get her weight down. Her weight of 186 pounds not only looked bad, but it also made Yvonne tired all the time. For someone only 5′ 4″ tall, that was a lot of excess weight to have to carry around all day. No wonder she felt tired—and looked it!

Yvonne had tried some other diets without success, but this time she was determined that she would stay on her diet until she was the thin person she used to be. Following my Amazing 600 Calorie Model's Diet, Yvonne won back her former figure of 117 pounds within five and a half months. Eating meals she enjoyed, she was still able to take off 69 pounds at the rate of about 3 pounds a week. Besides the fact that she's now much more slender, Yvonne looks a lot younger today!

I know that counting calories can be troublesome, so I'm going to make counting your calories easy for you. In this chapter I've done all the work for you. Here are my suggestions for setting up a 600-calorie-a-day menu for one whole month. I've listed breakfasts, lunches and dinners separately so that you can put together whatever combinations best fit your tastes and still have meals that add up to no more than 600 calories.

If you normally skip breakfast and want to continue to do so, go ahead; it'll give you that many more calories to spend on lunch and dinner. I don't like to see anyone skipping breakfast, but if you are one of those people who just can't break the no-breakfast habit, I won't force it on you. Some people like to eat their largest meal at lunch, with a smaller evening meal. Those that have this habit should select meals from the lunches that have a higher calorie count for more satisfaction, making sure to save enough calories for dinner, too. To supplement the menus for these situations, use my calorie counting lists in Chapter 9.

HOW TO MAKE UP YOUR SHOPPING LIST

Do your menu planning once a week and make up a shopping list from it. To be sure you cook meals that are fat-free, get yourself a frying pan with a surface such as Teflon which doesn't require the use of any fat or margarine. Buy yourself a postal scale for weighing your food portions. How else will you discover what 2 or 4 ounces of anything looks like? Get used to using a measuring cup and spoons so that your portions will be correct.

Explore the dietetic foods section of your supermarket. During your diet, you'll be eating dietetic fruit, salad dressings, gelatins, jams, chocolate syrup, pancake syrup and puddings. If you normally shop in only one store, investigate now what is being offered in other stores in the way of specialized foods that are low in calories.

Always read the label of any food container for the calorie count. Don't take it for granted that a food is low in calories just because it is in the dietetic food section. Many foods are there because they are free of sugar, salt or fat.

Always sit down when you eat and present your food as attractively as possible on a small plate. Don't have your beverage with your meal. Have it afterwards in the living room and drink it slowly, whatever it is.

I've tried to make up the menus with simple foods that are easy to measure. It is hard to get an accurate calorie count with many home-cooked recipes because every cook makes a meat loaf or stew differently and with different calorie counts. This is not the time to have to learn how to cook new recipes. That comes after you've lost your weight and want to start preparing low-calorie meals that will maintain your ideal weight and keep you from gaining again. I am presently working on a dieter's low-calorie cookbook which should be of tremendous help to anyone watching his or her weight. Measuring your food at all times is a must and will become a natural habit after a while and not seem like any trouble at all. Don't tell me that all this sounds like too much trouble. Nothing is too much trouble if you can have your slender figure back again.

You may have any of the following beverages, at any time during the day, as often as you like: tea and coffee without milk or cream, water, low-calorie drinks of all kinds. When you feel hungry, have something to drink and tell yourself you're just thirsty! It works.

COMMON MEASUREMENTS

	Equivalent	*Weight in ounces*
1½ teaspoons	½ Tablespoon	¼ fluid ounce
3 teaspoons	1 Tablespoon	½ fluid ounce
¼ cup	4 Tablespoons	2 ounces
⅓ cup	5 Tablespoons plus 1 teaspoon	4½ ounces (approximately)
⅜ cup	¼ cup plus 1 Tablespoon	2½ ounces
⅝ cup	½ cup plus 2 Tablespoons	5 ounces
⅞ cup	¾ cup plus 2 Tablespoons	7 ounces
1 cup	16 Tablespoons or ½ pint	8 ounces (approximately)
1 pint	2 cups	1 pound (approximately)
1 quart	2 pints or 4 cups	2 pounds (approximately)
1 ounce	28.35 grams	
1 pound	16 ounces or .454 kilograms	

Now let's look at a variety of breakfasts, lunches and dinners— meals for a whole month. Choose from among these the meals you'll find most appealing.

BREAKFASTS FOR A 600 CALORIE DIET

Selection	Calories
½ cup orange juice	60
½ cup skim milk	45
1 small egg, fixed to your preference	75
	180

1 glass (8 ozs.) Fit 'n Frosty chocolate drink	70
¾ oz. cheddar cheese	84
1 slice Gluten bread	35
	189

⅔ cup Wheatena cereal	100
½ cup skim milk	45
½ banana, sliced over cereal	44
	189

1 cup fresh cherries	82
1 cup skim milk	90
	172

2 scrambled eggs	150
1 navel orange	61
	211

3 ozs. low-calorie cranberry juice, with 3 ozs. orange juice	45
1 small poached egg	75
1 slice Gluten toast	35
	155

1 slice Pepperidge cinnamon raisin bread	76
2 tablespoons cottage cheese	34
	110

1 cup Kellogg's Sugar Frosted Flakes	144
½ cup skim milk	45
	189

½ cup cooked oatmeal	60

½ cup skim milk 45

½ banana.. 44

149

1 scrambled egg.................................. 80

1 slice Canadian bacon........................... 58

138

1 scrambled egg.................................. 80

1 slice bacon.................................... 49

½ fresh tomato.................................. 17

146

1 cup puffed rice 51

½ cup skim milk 45

½ cup blueberries 42

138

1 cup beef soup (canned) 100

4 rye wafer crackers.............................. 100

200

1 cup Quaker Puffed Wheat cereal 43

½ cup skim milk 45

8 ozs. orange juice............................... 99

187

½ cup All Bran cereal 96

½ cup skim milk 45

1 fresh peach 35

176

1 poached egg 77

1 slice Gluten bread 35

112

1 cup Alba 66 hot cocoa mix with water 60

1 slice raisin toast (Thomas's English).............. 66

126

1 cup Quaker Puffed Rice 51

½ banana   44
½ cup skim milk   45
                                                                          140

1 cup Kellogg's Special K.   70
½ cup skim milk   45
6 ozs. apple juice.   83
                                                                          198

1 slice Hollywood bread   46
1 small egg, soft boiled   75
¼ canteloupe   29
                                                                          150

1 scrambled egg.   80
1 slice bacon.   49
                                                                          129

1 cup Quaker Puffed Wheat   43
½ cup skim milk   45
½ banana   44
                                                                          132

2 ozs. roast beef.   156
1 slice whole wheat bread   56
½ grapefruit.   52
1 tablespoon Dia-Mel blackberry preserves   6
                                                                          270

1 cup chicken noodle soup   65
6 Chicken-in-a-Biskit crackers.   60
1 apple   66
                                                                          191

1 cooked link sausage.   95
1 scrambled egg.   75
                                                                          170

1 cup vegetable soup   77
6 Nabisco bacon-flavored Thins   66
½ cup fresh blackberries.   42
                                                                          185

1 cup Kellogg's Corn Flakes.   80
½ cup skim milk   45
½ banana   44
                                                                           169

1 cup tomato soup   88
4 Saltine crackers   48
½ cup skim milk   45
                                                                           181

1 cup green pea soup, canned   130
10 Cheeze-it crackers.   60
                                                                           190

1 navel orange   61
¼ cup cottage cheese   60
1 slice Gluten toast   35
                                                                           156

LUNCHES FOR A 600 CALORIE DIET

1 slice Gluten bread   35
1 slice cheese   100
1½ teaspoon mustard   6
6 ozs. skim milk.   66
½ cup D-Zerta lime gelatin   8
                                                                           215

½ frankfurter   76
2 slices tomato   8
¼ cup cottage cheese   60
½ cup D-Zerta lemon gelatin   8
                                                                           152

1 whole package Cantonese style Stir and Fry frozen
   vegetables (Bird's Eye)   90

1 oz. ham, cut up.   67
½ cup green pea soup, put ham in soup   65
2 round Melba Toast, garlic flavored, Old London brand. .   18
                                                                           150

½ cup Dannon plain yogurt   65
6 slices cucumber   7
1 fresh peach   35
                                                                      107

½ cup low fat cottage cheese   130
1 apple   66
                                                                      196

4 ozs. canned crabmeat   116
tomato shell   10
½ cup Diet Delight canned apricots   60
                                                                      186

1 egg, hard boiled   77
½ cup spinach   24
                                                                      101

4 ozs. canned crabmeat   116
salad of:
3 iceberg lettuce leaves   6
½ green pepper, chopped   7
1 oz. canned mushrooms   5
½ tomato   17
                                                                      151

½ cup low fat cottage cheese, mixed with: 130
½ green pepper, chopped   7
1 small radish, sliced   2
1 tablespoon raw onion, chopped   4
½ slice pumpernickel bread   37
                                                                      180

2 eggs   150
in omelette with:
4 ozs. canned mushrooms   19
5 sprigs watercress   1
                                                                      170

Vegetable plate of:
½ cup cauliflower   13
¼ cup peas   57
1 medium carrot   21

½ cup yellow squash............................... 16
½ cup broccoli 27
½ cup green beans 16
½ cup beets 31
                                                   181

⅛" slice of bologna 86
1 oz. longhorn cheese 112
4 Triangle Thin crackers........................... 32
                                                   230

1 slice Gluten bread 35
1 slice cheese 100
1½ teaspoons mustard 6
    (Spread bread with mustard, place cheese on   141
    top, broil in oven.)

1 cup beef broth.................................. 26
1 slice pumpernickel bread........................ 74
½ tablespoon margarine........................... 51
                                                   151

1 whole package Pennsylvania style frozen vegetables
    (Bird's Eye)................................... 120

1 egg, hard boiled................................ 77
1 medium tomato................................. 33
                                                   110

½ cup low fat cottage cheese...................... 130
½ canteloupe 58
                                                   188

6 broiled shrimp.................................. 64
3 iceberg lettuce leaves........................... 6
1 tomato 33
                                                   103

½ cup oyster stew, made with skim milk 78
10 Oysterette crackers 30
1 apple 80
                                                   188

1 whole package Japanese style Stir and Fry frozen
   vegetables (Bird's Eye)............................. 105

½ cup low fat cottage cheese........................ 130
1 slice fresh pineapple, 3½" X ¾"................... 44
½ cup strawberry D-Zerta gelatin 8
                                                   182

1 glass (8 ozs.) Fit 'n Frosty chocolate drink 70
1 slice Gluten bread 35
1 tablespoon imitation margarine.................... 50
                                                   155

4 ozs. broiled fish................................. 100
½ tomato.. 17
½ cucumber 15
½ cup orange D-Zerta gelatin 8
                                                   140

4 ozs. lobster..................................... 108
Salad of:
3 leaves iceberg lettuce............................ 6
½ tomato.. 17
2 tablespoons Featherweight French dressing 28
                                                   159

½ package New Orleans style frozen vegetables (Bird's
   Eye) 105
½ cup strawberry D-Zerta gelatin 8
                                                   113

4 ozs. broiled chicken 200
½ cup beets 27
½ cup string beans 16
½ cup lime D-Zerta gelatin 8
                                                   251

½ cup low fat cottage cheese........................ 130
1 cup strawberries 56
                                                   186

1 whole package Mandarin style Stir and Fry frozen
   vegetables (Bird's Eye)............................. 150

Salad of:

3 leaves iceberg lettuce	6
½ medium tomato	17
¼ green pepper	4
¼ cucumber	7
¾ oz. Swiss cheese, chopped	78
2 ozs. tuna	72
2 tablespoons Featherweight French dressing	28
	212

DINNERS FOR A 600 CALORIE DIET

3 ozs. beef tenderloin	136
½ cup spinach	23
1 tomato, sliced	33
½ cup strawberry D-Zerta gelatin	8
	200

4 ozs. lobster	108
½ cup fresh broccoli, cooked	20
2 radishes	4
½ cup cooked carrots	23
½ cup orange D-Zerta gelatin, topped with:	8
3 tablespoons D-Zerta whipped topping mix	24
	187

4 ozs. broiled fish	100

Salad made of:

3 leaves iceberg lettuce	6
1 medium tomato	17
2 tablespoons Featherweight French dressing	28
	151

3 ozs. roast turkey	150
1 tablespoon cranberry sauce	25
½ cup green peas	57
	232

1 small pork chop	100
¼ cup applesauce	25
½ cup chopped broccoli, frozen (Bird's Eye)	27
½ sliced tomato	17
	169

2 ozs. corned beef 200
1 cup cooked cabbage.............................. 34
½ cup red raspberries 35
                                                    ───
                                                    269

2 ozs. beef liver 65
3 tablespoons chopped onions 12
½ cup brussels sprouts in cheese sauce (Green Giant).... 85
½ cup carrots 23
½ cup lime D-Zerta gelatin 8
                                                    ───
                                                    193

½ package Japanese style Stir and Fry frozen vegetables
    (Bird's Eye)...................................... 53
Milkshake made of:
8 ozs. skim milk................................. 89
½ cup fresh strawberries............................ 28
2 ice cubes
¼ teaspoon vanilla
Low calorie sweetener
                                                    ───
                                                    170

1 small pork chop 100
¼ cup applesauce 25
½ cup carrots 23
½ green pepper, cut in strips 7
½ cup strawberry D-Zerta gelatin 8
                                                    ───
                                                    163

4 ozs. chicken liver................................. 94
Salad made of:
3 leaves iceberg lettuce............................. 6
½ tomato.. 17
¼ green pepper 4
3 small green onions, bulbs and tops, chopped 11
2 tablespoons Featherweight French dressing 28
                                                    ───
                                                    160

1 whole package Cantonese style Stir and Fry frozen
    vegetables (Bird's Eye)............................ 90
½ cup vanilla D-Zerta vanilla pudding 70
⅓ banana, sliced, folded into pudding................. 29
                                                    ───
                                                    189

4 ozs. broiled fish	100
Salad made of:	
3 leaves iceberg lettuce	6
½ cucumber	15
¼ green pepper	4
1 medium tomato	17
2 tablespoons Featherweight French dressing	28
	218

½ cup frozen broccoli, cauliflower, and carrots, in cheese sauce (Green Giant)	70
4 ozs. broiled fish	100
	170

4 ozs. broiled fish	100
1 baked tomato	34
½ cup broccoli, boiled and drained	20
½ cup blackberries	42
	196

3 ozs. chicken, white meat	156
½ cup green beans	16
½ cup carrots	23
	195

4 ozs. broiled fish	100
½ cup green beans	22
1 wedge (2″) honeydew melon	49
10 grapes	35
	206

½ package Mandarin style Stir and Fry frozen vegetables (Bird's Eye)	75
½ cup canned crabmeat, drained	86
½ cup fresh peach slices	33
	194

½ cup baby peas, pearl onions, and carrots in butter sauce (Green Giant)	80
2 strips bacon	98
1 Krispy cracker	12
	190

4 ozs. broiled fish.   100
½ cup beets, boiled, drained, and diced   27
½ cup spinach   24
                                                                          151

⅓ package Hawaiian style frozen vegetables, (Bird's Eye).   40
6 broiled shrimp.   64
½ cup fresh sweet cherries   41
                                                                          145

6 broiled shrimp on: 64
3 leaves iceberg lettuce.   6
½ cup cottage cheese   120
½ cup strawberry D-Zerta gelatin   8
                                                                          198

3 ozs. chicken, white meat   156
10 small leaves endive.   5
1 medium tomato.   35
                                                                          196

3 ozs. chicken, white meat   156
½ cup canned beets.   43
                                                                          199

4 ozs. broiled fish.   100
6 asparagus spears   19
½ cup unsweetened applesauce   49
                                                                          168

1 whole package Pennsylvania style frozen vegetables
   (Bird's Eye).   120
½ cup D-Zerta chocolate pudding   70
                                                                          190

3 ozs. chicken, white meat   156
½ cup turnip greens   15
½ tomato.   17
½ cup orange D-Zerta gelatin   8
                                                                          196

4 ozs. broiled fish.   100
1 baked tomato   34
½ broccoli, boiled.   20
½ cup blackberries. . . . .   <u>42</u>
                                                                                         196

1 whole package New Orleans style frozen vegetables
(Bird's Eye).   210

ADDITIONAL LOW-CALORIE FOODS

If you find, when planning your menu for the day, that you have less than 600 calories, you may add any of the following low-calorie foods:

Fruit

1 dried apricot (10)
1 candied cherry (17)
1 Maraschino cherry (10)
1 T. lemon juice (4)
1 strawberry(4)
1 T. lime juice (4)
½ fresh lemon (10)
½ fresh lime (10)
1 large dried prune (19)
4 grapes (10)

½ cup Diet Delight pears (60)
½ cup Diet Delight apricots (60)
½ cup Diet Delight peaches (50)
½ cup Diet Delight purple plums (70)
½ cup Diet Delight pineapple chunks (70)
½ cup Tillie Lewis applesauce (60)

Vegetables

¼ cup green beans (8)
¼ cup asparagus (9)
¼ cup wax beans (8)
¼ cup beet greens (9)
¼ cup broccoli (10)
¼ cup raw red cabbage (8)
¼ cup raw Chinese cabbage (4)
½ cup cauliflower (13)
1 stalk celery (6)
½ cup Swiss chard (14)
1 T. raw, chopped chives (3)

3 leaves iceberg lettuce (6)
3 leaves Romaine (5)
2 ozs. mushrooms (10)
½ mustard greens (16)
1 large green olive (5)
1 large Mission olive (8)
1 T. raw chopped onion (4)
3 small green (bulb and white part) onions (11)
1 T. chopped parsley (2)
½ tomato (17)

6 slices cucumber (7)
¼ cup boiled eggplant (10)
7 small leaves escarole (5)
¼ cup kohlrabi (10)
1 radish (2)

½ green pepper (7)
¼ cup summer squash (8)
¼ cup turnips (9)
¼ cup turnip greens (8)
5 sprigs watercress (1)

Nuts

1 almond (7)
1 filbert (8)
2 peanuts (10)

1 pecan half (9)
3 pistachio nuts (9)

Crackers

1 Nabisco bacon-flavored
    Thin (11)
3 Cheez-its (18)
1 Chicken-in-a-Biskit (10)
1 Chipper (14)
4 croutons (20)
1 Hi-Ho (17)
1 Krispy (12)
1 double square Rye-Krisp (20)

1 wheat or rye thin (10)
1 white round Melba Toast (8)
1 Triangle Thin (8)
1 Wheat Melba Toast (16)
1 Sociable (10)
3 Oysterettes (9)
1 saltine (12)
1 Ritz (18)

Desserts

½ cup D-Zerta gelatin (lime, orange, strawberry, lemon) (10)
½ cup D-Zerta pudding (vanilla, chocolate) (70)
1 tablespoon D-Zerta Whipped Topping Mix (8)
1 butterscotch hard candy (16)
1 jelly bean (8)
1 lemon drop (15)
1 Lifesaver (9)
1 small lollipop (20)
1 Kraft jet marshmallow (18)
1 after-dinner mint (12)
1 sourball (20)
1 animal cracker (8)
1 Arrowroot cookie (15)
1 chocolate snap (18)
1 chocolate wafer (13)
1 small gingersnap (17)

1 graham cracker (17)
1 lemon snap (17)
1 vanilla wafer (18)

Miscellaneous

1 bouillon cube (5)
5 small pretzel sticks (20)
1 T. creamed cottage cheese (17)
1 T. A-1 sauce (15)
1 T. barbecue sauce (17)
1 T. chili sauce (18)
1 T. hot pepper sauce (3)
1 T. meat sauce (10)
1 T. soy sauce (9)
1 T. tomato sauce (5)
1 T. thin white sauce (19)
1 T. Worcestershire sauce (15)
1 T. Featherweight pancake syrup (12)
1 T. Featherweight French dressing (14)
1 T. Featherweight Creamy Italian dressing (18)
1 T. Dia-Mel apricot preserves (6)
1 T. Dia-Mel apple jelly (6)
1 T. Dia-Mel blackberry preserves (6)
1 T. Dia-Mel grape jelly (6)
1 T. Dia-Mel marmalade (6)
2 t. Smucker's Slenderella strawberry jam (16)
1 T. Dia-Mel cherry preserves (6)
1 T. Dia-Mel peach preserves (6)

8

Some Hints for
Staying on Your Diet

Because you need all the help you can get to keep you on your diet, I will present in this chapter a potpourri of tips that I've found useful for myself.

Pick the right time to start your diet. This is very important because you don't want to be under any unusual strain or emotional stress. You should start on a day when you have no planned social activities, so weekends are out. Monday isn't a good day to start because too many little things have to be taken care of on Mondays. Tuesday through Thursday are the best days to begin. Get rid of any cookies, snacks and other fattening foods on Monday. Don't accept any luncheon or dinner invitations for a while until you are sure you can control your appetite and only order low-calorie food from the menu.

HOW FRIENDS CAN HELP

Try to get a friend to diet with you so you can compare notes. Find people who have been overweight before, but who are currently practicing weight control so that you can discuss your problems with them. This will reinforce your positive thoughts about losing weight.

Get your friend who is dieting to exercise with you at regular times each day. Try to get a group together if you can, for this will make exercise time pass faster and be more enjoyable. If you have the time and can afford it, join a health spa and pay in advance so that you'll feel like a spendthrift if you miss a session. It's always good for you to be around other people who are trying to correct their weight problems. Try not to spend time with overweight people unless they are dieting too, as it will have a negative effect on your thinking.

Do your food shopping alone and do it the day before you start your diet. Buy a large selection of diet drinks, fruit juices and low-calorie snacks so that you'll be well fortified for any appetite emergency. Canned fruit can be made into the low-calorie version by simply pouring off the heavy sweet syrup and washing it with water. This will also save you money since the low-calorie food is usually priced higher than regular food. Buy several kinds of non-caloric sweeteners such as saccharin tablets, liquid sweetener for cooking and sweetening your cold drinks and the granule kind for cereals. Always carry some non-caloric sweetener in your purse. While you're out shopping, steer clear of any bakery windows or ice cream parlors. Also, if you can get someone else in the family to do the shopping for you, take advantage of this. Don't read the food ads; they'll only whet your appetite. Try not to even think about food. Good snacks to stock up on for emergency hungers are carrots, dill or sweet pickles and tomatoes.

Buy a scale to weigh your food. This will help you to learn what 1 ounce of cheese or 2½ ounces of fish look like. If you like milk, drink fresh skim milk or evaporated skim milk diluted with water instead of whole milk because it has about half as many calories. I've discovered that canned skim milk doesn't taste as bad as it sounds. Flavor it with some saccharin and a teaspoon of vanilla. Throw in a few ice cubes and mix in a blender and you have yourself a delightful milkshake.

GETTING YOURSELF THROUGH EACH DAY

Diet one day at a time. Get yourself through "just this one day." Be patient. Remember that it took a long time to put on all that weight and you just can't get slim overnight no matter what all those advertisements say. Get more sleep. You'll have more willpower if you feel rested. Try to walk more. Take a look around your neighborhood in the early morning or after supper. Observe the patterns in the leaves of the trees, a flower, the song of a bird singing. Greet whomever you meet with a smile and a warm hello. If you don't like to walk, get a bicycle and ride it every day for at least 30 minutes to an hour. When you go out in the morning to pick up your paper from the lawn, bend down without bending your knees, then do a few deep breathing exercises, taking advantage of the fresh early morning air. Never feel sorry for yourself because you are on a diet. Try to appear happier than you are. Take some dancing lessons. There must be some steps you've always wanted to learn.

Take one of your fat, full-length photos and cut it out like a paper doll, cutting off the excess pounds to see how you will look when you lose that weight. Paste it up beside some of your fat photos.

Try doing something different with your hair to perk up your morale. A day spent at the beauty salon for the "whole works" will raise your spirits and make you feel like a worthwhile person.

Weigh yourself every day and measure your bust, waist, hips and thighs every three weeks, recording all information. In the morning you usually weigh less so choose that for your weigh-in time. Try to work on improving your posture. When you stand correctly, you always look thinner. Set smaller goals of 5 pounds at a time instead of going for your long-range goal of weight loss all at once. It'll make you feel like a winner instead of a failure. If you reach a dieting plateau and can't seem to lose any more weight, fast for one day and then resume your diet. Reward yourself with a little money as you lose each pound. Depending on what you can afford, put this sum into an envelope marked "reward" and when you have lost enough to buy some clothes in one size smaller, use this money to buy a new article of clothing. Buy a tape measure and cut it off at the place where you want your waist to measure and then measure yourself each morning until it meets. Buy a pair of jeans in one size smaller and try them on every week to see if you can close the zipper and button the top button. When you have reached your goal of lost weight, give away or throw out all of your larger-sized clothes so that there will be no turning back in the future. Find lots of things to keep you busy every minute so you won't have time to think about food.

WHAT TO WEAR

Don't wear baggy clothes when you exercise. Wear a form-fitting leotard instead. Baggy clothes not only make you feel frumpy and fat, but will prevent you from noticing any progress in your weight loss. Exercise to music that has a strong beat and it won't seem like such a chore. Take up some sport to inject more exercise and interest into your life. Start "thinking thin" at all times and accepting the idea that you will appear younger and more attractive when you lose your unwanted weight.

As you drive your car, tighten your abdominal muscles by pulling your stomach in, holding it for a few seconds and then letting it out. Exercise while talking on the phone. Just lift one leg straight up and parallel to the floor, as high as you can, and then lower it. Repeat with the other leg. Exercise your toes and feet by putting several marbles on the floor and picking them up with your toes. Roll the sole of your foot back and forth over several marbles. Use both feet together to pick up one or more marbles. Do these exercises while you are reading or watching television. Exercise at night before bedtime. Afterwards, take a shower to put yourself in the mood for a good night's sleep.

Get a nice tan all over your body, even if you have to use a sunlamp in the privacy of your home. Flab doesn't look as sickening when it has a little color to it. You'll look healthier too. Never, never eat while you are doing something else, such as reading or watching a movie or television. Take the time to enjoy the small portions of food you will be eating. Make eating a ritual to be appreciated more. Before you remove your makeup at night, look at your nude body, in front of your full-length mirror, and see if you are improving. Start wearing filmy, sexy nightgowns even if you sleep alone. Think of yourself as feminine and glamorous. Buy yourself a new bikini and wear it as soon as you're able.

THINKING ABOUT OTHER THINGS

Compliment someone every day. You'll feel better for it and people around you will respect you. If you think about food too much, because you have too much time on your hands, take up a new hobby. Study the fashion magazines and visualize how you might look in the latest styles.

When you turn down a sweet that's offered to you, you don't have to mention that you're on a diet. Just say that you have a tooth that's bothering you and you'll have to pass it up this time.

When you're dieting, it's always best to keep away from social activities that might bring you offers of snacks, food or cocktails, but if you're out with friends and everybody is ordering pizza, you can order some too, but pick off the sausage and eat that first, nibbling on the dough and leaving most of it. Fill up on a diet cola. Don't ever drink mixed drinks; they have too many calories. Your best bet is wine. If you usually drink one alcoholic beverage per day, cut it out and save 150 calories a day or 15 excess pounds per year. When you're out, always carry a pocket-sized calorie counter with you. Before you order in a restaurant, ask the waiter not to bring any bread or butter to the table. Out of sight, out of mind! Never eat more than two bites of any dessert. Eat slowly at all times, and chew your food thoroughly. Never eat standing up. Carry sugarless gum with you at all times.

Which foods do you hate the most? Keep one or more on hand so that when you feel tempted to break your diet rules, you can ask yourself, "Am I hungry enough to eat that?" If you're not really hungry and it's time for dinner, don't eat out of habit. Tell yourself that you will wait until later. Later, you may not be hungry at all.

Don't use sugar in your beverages. Every teaspoonful has 18 calories. Eat alone or with another dieter. Whenever you feel yourself getting hungry at the wrong times, say to yourself, "I'm not hungry, I'm really only thirsty." Then get yourself a glass of no-calorie soda or a hot cup of tea or coffee. If you have no beverage on hand, drink either ice water or hot water. One day a week try using only liquids. Omit salt or use it sparingly. Unsalted foods are less tempting and you will eat less of them. Remember that a bouillon cube in a cup of hot water has only 5 calories, but can seem very filling because of its good taste.

Go shopping and look at all the clothes in one size smaller than what you are wearing now. Shop in the diet foods section of the grocery store so that you can eat more while consuming fewer calories. If you can talk someone else into making the meals this week, do it. Go food shopping when you're not hungry. Always make a list. Get into the habit of drinking more water. Be sure you get some vitamin C each day because it cannot be stored in your body. Always brush your teeth after you eat. It dulls your urge to eat anything immediately afterward.

Keep your head when eating in restaurants. Skip the creamed soups and order the shrimp cocktail. Don't eat any fried food. Pass up the rolls, gravy, butter, sour cream, potatoes and bread (and, naturally, any dessert should be avoided because you don't have a large enough calorie count to work with.) Never eat white bread again. Instead of a cocktail before dinner, try a hot cup of bouillon soup. Eat more fruit and vegetables than you have been eating, and also more salad greens. Always carry Life Savers in your purse for emergency cravings.

Learn how to decalorize your favorite recipes and when you are cooking for the family, try to use low-calorie foods. Try eating some foods you thought you disliked, to keep from overeating. Who knows? You may even get to like them. Use seasonings to perk up the taste of food. Chopped parsley and chives make plain potatoes taste better. Monosodium glutamate makes vegetables, fish and lean meats more delicious and lemon juice is a good flavoring to use on lots of dishes. Try sprinkling fresh mint leaves on boiled carrots for a new taste sensation. Try to get used to eating bread without margarine or butter. It doesn't taste as bad as you think it will and you'll appreciate the subtle flavoring of cracked, whole wheat and rye bread more. Plan your menus so that you won't be tempted to eat at the wrong times. Drink a no-calorie soda before eating a solid food to fill up your stomach.

Serve fish often. It has fewer calories and is less expensive than meat. Use low-calorie salad dressings and save on calories. To cut down on calories, use yogurt instead of sour cream. When you eat a piece of fruit, don't just eat it the way it is; cut it into small pieces and eat it with a fork on the fanciest dish you own. Use evaporated skim milk to make imitation whipped cream. A tablespoon only contains 3 calories, whereas real whipped cream contains 50 calories. Always cut off all visible fat before preparing meat.

Have a glamour photograph made of yourself posing in a new bikini, showing off your new figure. Now that you're thin again, keep a jar of hard candy on hand for those times when you can't resist the urge to eat something.

A COUPLE WHO HELPED EACH OTHER

The Amazing 600 Calorie Model's Diet is not just for women. It works just as well for men. Darlene T. came to me for advice on how to get her husband Jeff to take off some weight. Jeff had tried several other diets, but he never seemed to be able to stay on them for long enough to do much good. Darlene was about 15 pounds overweight, so I suggested to her that she go on a diet with her husband so that he wouldn't feel alone and deprived when he ate. Jeff was cooperative as long as someone else was planning the meals and counting the calories, and he agreed that if Darlene joined him, dieting together would give him the willpower to continue until he had lost the 30 pounds he needed to shed. Instead of going out to lunch as he used to, Jeff ate the lunch Darlene packed for him every day (with an encouraging love note tucked inside the paper napkin) of a hard boiled egg, three cherry tomatoes and a piece of fruit. She'd vary this on other days with ½ cup of low-fat cottage cheese and a fresh peach or 3 ounces of broiled chicken (skinned) and a salad of greens, tomato and low-calorie dressing. She packed the dressing separately in a discarded pill bottle so that the greens would not become withered. Darlene lost her 15 pounds in six weeks and Jeff lost his excess 30 pounds in 15 weeks. They both delight in telling others about my Amazing 600 Calorie Model's diet every time someone remarks how well they look. They are both proud as peacocks with themselves!

9

Calories in Popular Foods

Use the lists of foods in this chapter to keep your meals within the 600 calorie limit. You will find that a lot of variety is possible with this diet.

Here is some general information about the lists that follow. Measurements of spoonsful, cups, and so on are all *level*.

Equivalent Measurements

1 Tablespoon = 3 teaspoons	1 cup = ½ pint liquid
4 Tablespoons = ¼ cup	2 cups = 1 pint
5⅓ Tablespoons = ⅓ cup	2 pints (4 cups) = 1 quart
8 Tablespoons = ½ cup	4 quarts = 1 gallon
12 Tablespoons = ¾ cup	16 ounces = 1 pound
16 Tablespoons = 1 cup	1 ounce = 28.35 grams
1 fluid ounce = 2 Tablespoons	

Abbreviations in the Lists

dia. = diameter	" = inch
oz. = ounce	pkg. = package
lb. = pound	swt. = sweetened
qt. = quart	unswt. = unsweetened
T. = tablespoon	w/ = with
tsp. = teaspoon	w/o = without
C. = cup	

CALORIE COUNTDOWN

Selection *Calories*

Abalone,
    canned, 4 ozs. 91
    raw, 5″ x 6″ x ¼″ 100

Alcoholic beverages—See separate listing at end of chapter.

Almonds,
    blanched (Blue Diamond) ½ oz. 88
    chocolate covered, 1 nut 14
    dry roasted (Franklin) ½ oz. 77
    dry roasted (Planters) ½ oz. 90
    roasted and salted, 1 nut 8
    roasted and unsalted, 1 nut 7

Ambrosia,
    ½ cup 80
    Kraft, 4 ozs. 87

Anchovies, canned, 5 fillets 35

Anchovy paste, 1 tsp. 15

Apple brown betty, ¼ cup 88

Apple butter, 1 T. 37

Apple drink, canned, Hi-C, 6 ozs. 87

Apple-grape drink, Welch's, 6 ozs. 93

Apple juice, canned,
    Heinz, 6 ozs. 81
    Mott's, 6 ozs. 84

Apple,
    baked, ½ apple w/ 1 T. brown sugar. 92
    raw, peeled, 2½″ dia. 66
    raw, unpeeled, 2½″ dia. 80
    dried, cooked, swt., ¼ cup 79
    dried, cooked, unswt., ¼ cup 51
    frozen slices (Mott's), swt., ½ cup 100

Applesauce,
    canned, swt., ½ cup 100
    canned, unswt., ½ cup 49

Apricot nectar, canned or bottled, 6 ozs. 100

Apricots,
    fresh, 3.. 55
    candied, 1 average 100
    4 halves with 2 T. heavy syrup..................... 100
    low-calorie, 4 or 5 halves 41
    dried, 1.. 10
    dried, cooked, swt., ¼ cup......................... 100
    dried, cooked, unswt., ¼ cup....................... 60
    frozen, swt., ¼ cup 64
    canned with juice pack, ½ cup with liquid 54
    canned with water pack, ½ cup with liquid 38

Artichoke hearts,
    canned, 5 25
    frozen (Bird's Eye), 4 44

Artichokes, French, drained, 1 average 53

Asparagus,
    boiled, drained,
        6 spears....................................... 19
        cut spears, ½ cup............................... 18
    canned,
        green, 6 spears................................. 20
        white, 6 spears................................. 21
    frozen,
        6 spears....................................... 23
        ½ cup of cuts and tips.......................... 21

Avocados,
    California, ¼ average.............................. 93
    Florida, ½ average 79

Bacon,
    broiled or fried, 1 slice 49

Canadian, broiled or fried, 1 slice 58

Bagel, ½ medium 63

Bamboo shoots, raw, 1 cup 40

Bananas,
    1 average, 6¾" long................................. 87
    ½ average, fried..................................... 56

Barracuda, 1½" x 1" x 1" 99

Bass,
    sea, raw, 3 ozs. 80
    smallmouth and largemouth, raw, 3 ozs. 89
    striped, raw, 3 ozs. 90
    white, raw, 3 ozs. 84

Bean sprouts,
    mung, raw, ½ cup 16
    soy, raw, ½ cup 25

Beans,
    baked with pork and molasses sauce, ¼ cup 99
    baked with pork and tomato sauce, canned, ¼ cup........ 80
    with tomato sauce, canned, ¼ cup 79

Beans and franks,
    (Campbell's) canned, 2 ozs. 92
    (Heinz) canned, 2 ozs. 93

Beans, barbecue, canned (Campbell's), 3 ozs.............. 93

Beans, green,
    boiled, drained, ½ cup 16
    canned, ½ cup with liquid........................... 21
    canned, drained, ½ cup.............................. 15
    cut in jars (Lord Mott's), ½ cup 15
    frozen, cut, ½ cup 22
    frozen, cut (Seabrook Farms), ½ cup 25
    frozen, whole (Bird's Eye), ½ cup 23
    frozen, French style with almonds (Bird's Eye), ½ cup..... 51
    frozen, French style with mushrooms (Bird's Eye), ½ cup .. 26

frozen, French style with mushroom sauce (Seabrook Farms),
½ cup 100

frozen with butter sauce (Bird's Eye), ½ cup 63

frozen Italian style (Bird's Eye), ½ cup 27

Beans, kidney, canned, ⅓ cup 77

Beans, lima,

boiled and drained, ½ cup........................... 89

canned, ½ cup with liquid........................... 82

canned, drained, ½ cup.............................. 77

frozen, baby, ⅓ cup................................. 76

frozen with butter sauce (Bird's Eye), ⅓ cup 78

frozen in cheese sauce (Seabrook Farms), ¼ cup.......... 70

Beans, wax,

boiled, drained, ½ cup 16

canned, ½ cup with liquid........................... 23

canned, drained, ½ cup............................. 18

frozen, cut, ½ cup 25

Beef,

boiled, 1 oz.. 62

braised, lean only, 2 ozs. 76

chuck roast, lean, 1 oz.............................. 63

club steak, lean, broiled, 1 oz. 70

filet mignon, 1 oz................................... 83

flank, 1 oz... 70

ground,

regular, 1 oz. 82

lean, 1 oz...................................... 63

porterhouse steak, lean, broiled, 1 oz. 71

rib, lean only, 1 oz................................. 69

round steak, lean only, 1 oz......................... 65

rump, lean only, roasted, 1 oz. 62

sirloin steak, lean only, 1 oz. 69

T-bone steak, lean only, 1 oz......................... 70

tenderloin, 1 oz.................................... 68

corned
    boiled, med. fat, 1 oz............................. 100
    canned, med. fat, 1 oz. 75
    canned, lean, 1 oz................................ 53

Beef goulash, canned (Heinz), 4 ozs..................... 94

Beef,
    potted, 1 oz.. 71
    roast, canned, 1 oz. 64
    stew meat, chuck, 1 oz............................. 100
    round roast, 1 oz.................................. 78

Beef and vegetable stew, 4 ozs. 90

Beef heart, see Heart.

Beef kidney, see Kidney.

Beef liver, see Liver.

Beef stew,
    (Heinz) 4 ozs. canned 91
    (Bounty) 4 ozs. canned 90
    (Dinty Moore) 4 ozs. canned 91
    (Armour Star) ½ cup, canned 100

Beef tongue, see Tongue.

Beet greens, boiled, drained, ½ cup..................... 18

Beets,
    boiled, drained, diced, ½ cup........................ 27
    canned, ½ cup with liquid.......................... 43
    canned, drained, ½ cup............................. 31
    diced, canned (Comstock), ½ cup.................... 41
    sliced, in jars (Lord Mott's), ½ cup 25
    pickled, in jars (Lord Mott's), ½ cup 63

Beverages, non-alcoholic, see Soft Drinks

Biscuit, ½ medium 65

Blackberries,
    fresh, ½ cup.. 42

canned, syrup pack, ⅓ cup with liquid 76

canned, water pack, ½ cup with liquid................. 43

frozen, sweetened, ½ cup 95

frozen, unsweetened, ½ cup 44

Blackberry juice, unsweetened, 1 cup..................... 66

Blintzes, ½ small..................................... 76

Blueberries,

fresh, ½ cup.. 42

canned, syrup pack, ¼ cup with liquid 63

canned, water pack, ½ cup with liquid................. 47

frozen, sweetened, ½ cup 95

frozen, unsweetened, ½ cup 44

Blueberry juice, unsweetened, ½ cup..................... 55

Blueberry pie, frozen (Banquet), ¹⁄₁₆ of a whole pie 92

Bluefish,

fresh or frozen, baked with 2 tsp. butter 83

fresh or frozen, broiled with 2 tsp. butter............... 91

Bologna,

all meat, 1 oz. 78

with cereal added, 1 oz. 75

⅛″ slice... 86

Bonito, 1½″ x 1″ x ¼″ 81

Bouillon cube, 1..................................... 5

Brains, all kinds, 1 oz. 36

Boysenberries,

canned, water pack, ½ cup with liquid................. 45

fresh, ¼ lb.. 63

frozen, unsweetened, ½ cup 32

Boysenberry pie, frozen (Banquet), ¹⁄₁₆ of a whole pie 86

Bran, see Cereals

Braunschweiger, 1 oz. 91

Brazil nuts, 1 nut..................................... 30

Bread,

Boston brown, 1 slice, 3″ x ¾″ 100

bran, 1 slice 75

corn, mix prepared (Aunt Jemima), 1″ x 1″ x ½″ 75

corn and molasses (Pepperidge Farm), 1 slice 63

cracked wheat, 1 slice (20 slices per loaf) 60

cracked wheat, (Pepperidge Farm), 1 slice 66

French, 1 slice, 3¼″ x 2″ x 1″ 58

French, brown and serve, baked (Pepperidge Farm), ¾″ slice   79

Gluten, 1 slice 35

Hollywood, 1 slice 46

Italian, 1 slice, 3½″ x 2″ x 1″ 55

low-starch (Arnold), 1 slice 46

oatmeal (Pepperidge Farm), 1 slice 66

Profile, 1 slice 52

protein, 1 slice 45

pumpernickel, 1 slice, 3¾″ x 3″ x ⅛″ 74

pumpernickel (Pepperidge Farm), 1 slice 79

pumpernickel, 1 party slice, 3″ x 2″ x ½″ 37

raisin, 1 slice (20 per loaf) 60

raisin (Thomas's English), 1 slice 66

raisin cinnamon (Pepperidge), 1 slice 76

raisin cinnamon (Thomas's English), 1 slice 63

rye,

light, 1 slice (20 per loaf) 63

light, party slice, 3″ x 2″ x ½″ 36

Pepperidge Farm, 1 slice 88

Tasty-Bake, 1 slice 91

Vienna, 1 slice, 3¼″ x 2″ x 1″ 58

white, 1 slice (20 per loaf) 62

white, thin slice, (26 per loaf) 46

white, Wonder, 1 slice 66

whole wheat, 1 slice (20 per loaf) 56

whole wheat (Pepperidge Farm), 1 slice 66

Breadcrumbs, dry, grated, ¼ cup 86

Bread, sweet,

banana nut roll, canned (Dromedary), ½″ slice 71

brown bread, canned, with raisins (B&M), ½″ slice 90

chocolate nut roll, canned (Dromedary), ½″ slice 87

cinnamon, ½ slice 65

corn, ½ piece 65

date nut roll (Thomas's), 1 slice...................... 100

date nut (Dromedary) canned, ½″ slice................. 75

fruit and nut (Crosse & Blackwell), ½″ slice 77

orange nut, canned (Crosse & Blackwell), ½″ slice........ 76

orange nut, canned (Dromedary), ½″ slice............... 77

raisin, cinnamon (Pepperidge Farm), 1 slice............. 76

raisin, cinnamon (Thomas's), 1 slice................... 63

Breadstick... 40

Broccoli,

fresh, boiled, drained, cut spears, ½ cup............... 20

frozen, chopped, ½ cup............................. 27

frozen spears (Bird's Eye), 1 spear 26

frozen, chopped (Bird's Eye), ½ cup 27

frozen, chopped (Seabrook Farms), ½ cup 30

frozen spears in butter sauce (Bird's Eye), ½ cup 58

frozen, chopped in cream sauce (Bird's Eye), ¼ cup....... 59

Brussels sprouts,

fresh, boiled, drained, ½ cup 23

frozen (Bird's Eye), ½ cup 34

Buns,

cinnamon, ½ bun.................................. 79

cinnamon, raisin, ½ bun 92

hot cross, ½ bun 60

pecan, ½ bun 93

Butter, salted or unsalted,

1 T... 100

1 pat 50

Butterfish,

  gulf, raw, 3 ozs.................................... 81

  northern, raw, 2 ozs. 96

Buttermilk, see Milk

Butternuts, 4 or 5 nuts................................ 94

Cabbage,

  white, raw, shredded, ½ cup........................ 12

  white, boiled, drained, ½ cup....................... 17

  red, raw, ½ cup shredded 16

  Chinese, raw, shredded, ½ cup...................... 7

  spoon, boiled, drained, ½ cup 11

Cakes,

  angel food, 1½″ (¹⁄₁₆ of a 10″ round cake)................ 100

  applesauce, 1″ x 1″ x ½″ 100

  butter cake, plain without icing, 1″ x 1″ x 1″ 100

  chocolate cake with chocolate icing, 2 bites 100

  coconut, 1″ x 1″ x 1″................................. 85

  cupcake (from mix) without icing, 2½″ dia. 90

  cupcake (from mix) with chocolate icing, ½ cake......... 65

  devil's food, 1″ x 1″ x 1″ 75

  fruit, 1″ x 1″ x ¼″.................................. 65

  gingerbread, 1″ x 2″ x 2″............................ 100

  Lady Baltimore, 2″ x 1″ x ½″ 87

  one egg cake, 1″ x 1″ x 1″ 100

  pound, 1¼″ x 1½″ x ¼″ 70

  spice, 1″ x 1″ x 1″.................................. 95

  sponge, 1″ sector of an 8″ round cake.................. 60

  white, 1″ x 1″ x 1″ 78

Calves liver, see Liver

Candied fruit, see individual listings

Candies,

  Almond Joy, ¼ of a bar.............................. 62

  Almond Brittle (Kraft), ¼ oz......................... 60

Almond Cluster, ½ of a bar........................ 86

almond toffee (Kraft), chocolate covered, 1 piece 27

almond, chocolate candy-coated (Hershey), 1 piece........ 10

almonds, sugar coated, ½ oz......................... 64

bon-bon, 1 50

buttermint (Kraft), 1 piece........................... 8

butterscotch, 1″ x 1″ x ¼″ 16

caramel, chocolate (Kraft), 1 piece 32

caramel, vanilla (Kraft), 1 piece 33

caramelettes, 1 piece 12

Caravelle, ½ of a bar................................ 96

cashew cluster, chocolate-covered (Kraft), 1 piece 58

cherries, candied, 1 9

chocolate, bitter, ½ oz. 70

chocolate, milk (Hershey), ⅓ of a bar 89

chocolate, milk (Hershey), ⅓ of a bar 84

chocolate kisses (Hershey), 1 piece.................... 47

chocolate, semi-sweet, ½ oz. 73

chocolate, semi-sweet, ⅓ of a bar..................... 72

chocolate cream, 1 piece, 1¼″ x ¾″ 55

coconut, chocolate-covered, ½ oz. 61

coconut creams, 1, ¾″ in dia......................... 48

cream mint, 2 small................................. 50

fondant, 1 patty 39

fruit drops, 3 pieces................................ 100

fudge with nuts, ½ oz. 60

Fudgies, chocolate, 1 piece 34

glazed fruits, 1 oz.................................. 95

gum drops, 1 large, 1″ in dia. 49

jelly beans, 1 8

junior mints, 1 piece 8

Jujubes, 1 piece 2

Jujyfruit, 1 piece 9

Krackel, ⅓ of a bar 82

lemon drops, 1..................................... 15

licorice rope twist, 7½″ long.......................... 37
Life Savers, all flavors, 1 piece...................... 9
Life Saver mint, 1 piece 7
lollipops,
    1 small 20
    2″ in dia....................................... 100
marshmallow, 1 med, 1¼″ in dia. 26
marshmallow, jet (Kraft), 1 piece 18
marshmallow, chocolate-covered (Kraft), 1 piece.......... 31
mints,
    after-dinner, ½″ sq., 1 piece........................ 12
    chocolate, 1½″ dia., 1 piece..................... 90
    cream, 1 piece 22
Mounds, ¼ of a bar.................................. 68
Mr. Goodbar, ¼ of a bar 81
O Henry, ¼ of a bar 82
orange peel, candied, 1 piece, 1″ x 2″ x 2″ 41
peanut cluster, chocolate-covered (Kraft), 1 piece 20
peanut brittle,
    (Kraft), ½ oz.................................... 61
    1 piece, 2″ x 2″ x ¼″ 48
pecan praline, ¼ piece............................... 100
penuche, 1½″ cube.................................. 100
popcorn ball, 1..................................... 100
popcorn, sugared, ½ cup............................. 74
raisins, chocolate-covered, ½ oz. 60
sourballs, 1 piece 20
Sugar Baby, 1 piece................................. 4
Sugar Daddy, ½ piece 65
taffy, 1 piece....................................... 50
toffee (Kraft), chocolate, 1 piece...................... 34

Cantaloupe,
    fresh, ½ melon, 5″ dia............................. 58
    fresh, diced, ½ cup 36

Capers, 1 T.. 8

Carrots,
 1 raw, average, 5½″ x 1″ 21
 boiled, drained, diced, ½ cup......................... 23
 canned, ½ cup with liquid............................ 34
 canned, drained, ½ cup.............................. 23

Cashew nuts, roasted, salted or unsalted, 6 to 8 nuts 84

Catsup, tomato, bottled, regular, hickory or pizza flavor, 1 T. . 21

Cauliflower,
 boiled, drained, ½ cup 13
 frozen, ½ cup....................................... 21

Caviar,
 granular, 1 oz. 74
 pressed, 1 oz.. 89

Celery,
 raw, 1 outer stalk 6
 raw, diced, ½ cup 9
 boiled, drained, ½ cup 9

Cereals,
 All-Bran, ¼ cup..................................... 48
 Alpha-Bits, ½ cup 55
 Apple Jacks, ½ cup 56
 Bran, 100% (Nabisco), ½ cup......................... 75
 Bran flakes, 40% (Kellogg's), ½ cup 70
 Bran and prune flakes (Post), ½ cup.................. 60
 Bran and raisin flakes (General Mills), ½ cup............ 63
 Bran Buds, ¼ cup 49
 Cap'n Crunch, ½ cup 76
 Cheerios, ½ cup..................................... 50
 Cocoa Krispies, ½ cup 57
 Cocoa Puffs, ½ cup.................................. 56
 Concentrate, ¼ cup 80
 Corn flakes (Kellogg's), ½ cup 40
 Cream of Wheat, cooked, ½ cup 67
 Crispy Critters, ½ cup............................... 55

farina, regular, cooked, ½ cup 50

farina, instant-cooking, ½ cup 66

farina, quick-cooking, ½ cup 51

Froot Loops, ½ cup................................ 57

Frosty-O's, ½ cup 64

Grape Nuts, 2 T. 51

Jets, ½ cup....................................... 71

Kix, ½ cup....................................... 42

Krumbles, ½ cup.................................. 70

Life, ½ cup....................................... 71

Lucky Charms, ½ cup.............................. 49

Oat flakes (Post), ¼ cup 41

Oatmeal or rolled oats, cooked, ½ cup................ 60

OK's, ½ cup...................................... 41

Pep, ½ cup 53

Post Toasties, ½ cup 55

Product 19, ½ cup 53

puffed corn, ½ oz................................. 55

puffed rice (Quaker), 1 cup 51

puffed wheat (Quaker), 1 cup 43

Raisin Bran (Kellogg's), ½ cup...................... 75

Ralston, cooked, ¾ cup 94

Rice flakes, ½ cup................................. 59

Rice Honeys, ½ cup 76

Rice Krispies, ½ cup............................... 53

Shredded Wheat,

   1 biscuit (Kellogg's)............................... 62

   1 biscuit (Quaker)................................ 66

   spoon size (Nabisco), 9 biscuits 33

Special K, ½ cup.................................. 35

Stars, ½ cup...................................... 55

Stax, ½ cup 41

Sugar Crisps, ½ cup 74

Sugar Frosted Flakes, ½ cup........................ 72

Sugar Pops, ½ cup................................. 55

Sugar Smacks, ½ cup 55

Sugar Sparkled Flakes, ½ cup....................... 74

Sugar Sparkled Rice Krinkles, ½ cup................. 83

Total, ½ cup....................................... 83

Trix, ½ cup 56

Twinkles, ½ cup.................................... 64

wheat, rolled, cooked, ½ cup 44

Wheat Honeys, ½ cup 76

Wheatena, cooked, ⅓ cup........................... 50

Wheaties, ½ cup 54

Chard, Swiss,

    raw, 2 ozs.. 13

    cooked, ½ cup 14

Cheese,

    American, processed, ¾ oz.......................... 69

    American, Borden's, ¾ oz........................... 69

    American, Kraft, ¾ oz.............................. 69

    American, Kraft, Old English, ¾ oz. 69

    American, "Vera-Sharp," ¾ oz....................... 69

    blue or Roquefort type, ¾ oz. 69

    blue,

        Borden's Blufort Brand, ¾ oz. 78

        Borden's Danish, ¾ oz............................. 69

        Kraft, ¾ oz....................................... 75

    brick, ¾ oz... 69

    brick, natural (Kraft), ¾ oz. 69

    brick, natural, aged (Kraft Lagerkäse), ¾ oz. 81

    brick, processed (Kraft), ¾ oz....................... 77

    camembert (Borden's), 1 oz. 86

    camembert (Kraft), 1 oz............................ 85

    caraway (Kraft), ¾ oz.............................. 84

    cheddar,

        (Borden's), ¾ oz................................. 84

        (Borden's Longhorn), ¾ oz. 84

(Borden's Wisconsin Old Fashioned), ¾ oz. 84

(Kraft), ¾ oz. 84

Colby (Kraft), ¾ oz. 84

cottage, creamed,

¼ cup 60

1 oz. 30

1 T. 17

cottage, uncreamed,

½ cup 98

1 oz. 24

1 T. 14

cream cheese,

¾ oz. 78

1 T. 56

(Kraft), scant 1 oz. 100

edam (Kraft), ¾ oz. 78

Frankenmuth (Kraft), ¾ oz. 84

Gorgonzola (Kraft), ¾ oz. 84

gouda (Kraft), ¾ oz. 78

gruyere (Kraft), ¾ oz. 83

Liederkranz Brand, 1 oz. 86

limburger, 1 oz. 97

Monterey (Kraft), ¾ oz. 78

mozzarella (Kraft), 1 oz. 79

muenster (Kraft), 1 oz. 100

muenster, processed (Kraft), ¾ oz. 75

Neufchatel (Borden's), 1 oz. 71

Nuworld, ¾ oz. 78

Old English, processed, ¾ oz. 78

Parmesan, ¾ oz. 83

Parmesan, grated, 1T. 29

pimiento, American, processed, ¾ oz. 78

Port DuSalut (Kraft), 1 oz. 100

provolone, 1 oz. 99

ricotta, moist (Borden's), 1 oz. 42

Romano, ¾ oz. 83
Romano, grated, 1 T. 30
Roquefort, ¾ oz. 78
Swiss, domestic, ¾ oz. 78
Swiss, processed, 1 oz. 95
Swiss with American, processed (Kraft), 1 oz. 99
Swiss with Muenster, processed (Kraft), 1 oz. 98

Cheese Doodles (Old London), 10 pieces. 26

Cheese food, American, processed, 1 oz. 77

Cheese Puffs, frozen (Durkee), 1 piece. 40

Cheese spreads,
American, ½ oz. 41
American (Snack Mate), 1 oz. 84
American (Vera-Sharp), ¾ oz. 78
bacon (Borden's Cheese 'N' Bacon), 1 oz. 98
bacon (Kraft), 1 oz. 92
blue (Borden's Blue Brand), 1 oz. 82
Borden's Chateau, 1 oz. 92
cheddar (Snack Mate), 1 oz. 84
Cheez Whiz, 1 oz. 76
chive cream cheese (Kraft), ½ oz. 42
garlic (Kraft), 1 oz. 86
hickory smoke flavored (Borden's), ½ oz. 78
limburger, 1 oz. 70
olive-pimiento cream cheese (Kraft), ½ oz. 43
pimiento,
(Cheez Whiz Pimiento), 1 oz. 76
(Kraft), 1 oz. 77
(Sealtest), 1 oz. 77
(Snack-Mate), 1 oz. 90
(Velveeta Pimiento), 1 oz. 84
Velveeta, 1 oz. 84
Cheese Straws (Durkee), frozen, 1 piece 48

Cheese Twists, 5 pieces. 16

Cherries,

    sour, fresh, ½ cup 35

    sweet, fresh, ½ cup 41

    candied, 1 average 17

    canned, sour, heavy syrup, ¼ cup with liquid 58

    canned, sour, water pack, ½ cup with liquid 47

    canned, sweet, heavy syrup, ¼ cup with liquid........... 53

    canned, sweet, water pack, ½ cup with liquid........... 53

    frozen, sour, unsweetened, ½ cup...................... 61

    maraschino, bottled, 2 ozs. with liquid 66

    maraschino, bottled, 2 average 19

Cherry drink, (Hi-C), 6 ozs............................ 90

Chestnuts,

    fresh, 1 nut...................................... 10

    dried, shelled, ¼ cup............................... 94

Chewing gum, see Gum

Chicken,

    broiled, meat only, 2 ozs. 78

    roasted, dark meat, 1 oz............................. 53

    roasted, light meat, 1 oz............................. 52

    roasted, meat and skin, 1 oz. 71

    stewed, meat only, 1 oz. 60

    canned, boned, 1 oz................................ 57

    potted, 1 oz...................................... 71

Chicken gizzards, boiled, drained, 2 ozs. 84

Chicken liver, see Liver

Chicken noodle dinner, canned (Heinz), 4 ozs. 86

Chicken stew, canned (Bounty), 4 ozs. 93

Chicken stew with dumplings, canned (Heinz), 4 ozs. 94

Chicory, raw, 10 inner leaves........................... 5

Chili powder, 1 T. 50

Chili with beans, canned, ¼ cup 83

Chili without beans, canned, 3 T........................ 96

Chili sauce, tomato, bottled, 1 T. 18

Chips, etc., ½ oz.,

    Bows... 81

    Bugles.. 81

    Buttons 73

    Nabisco Sip 'N' Chips............................ 73

    Corn:

      Fritos 83

      Old London 75

      Old London Dipsy Doodles................... 75

      Wise 84

      barbecue flavored (Old London Bar-B-Q Doodles) 75

      barbecue flavored (Wise).......................... 81

    Potato

      Frito-Lay Ruffles 78

      Lay's... 78

      Wise 81

      Wise Ridgies 81

      barbecue flavored (Lays) 78

      barbecue flavored (Wise)...................... 81

      tortilla (Frito-Lay Doritos)................... 75

      tortilla (Old London) 61

    Puffs, cheese flavored or coated:

      Frito-Lay Chee Tos 80

      Nabisco Flings 85

      Nabisco Swiss 'n Ham Flings................... 74

      Nabisco Shapies.............................. 75

      Old London Cheese Doodles.................. 70

      Wise Cheese Pixies 80

      Wonder Cheese Twists........................ 73

    Puffs, corn flavored (Wonder Corn Sticks)............. 80

    Rinds, bacon, fried (Wonder) 70

    Rinds, pork, fried (Frito-Lay Bakenets)............... 75

    Rinds, pork, fried (Wise Bakon Delites) 84

    Rinds, pork, fried, barbecue flavored (Wise Bakon Delites). 81

Sticks, potato (Wise Julienne)........................ 69

Whistles 71

Chives, raw, chopped, 1 T. 3

Chocolate candy, see Candy

Chocolate syrups, see Syrups and Toppings

Chop suey, chicken (canned), ½ cup 55

Chop suey, beef (canned), 5 ozs. 43

Chow mein, ½ cup 75

Chutney, 1 T. 50

Cider, see Apple juice

Clam juice, 5 ozs. 45

Clams,

cherry stone, raw, 6................................ 65

hard or round, raw, meat only, 4 ozs.................. 91

soft, raw, meat only, 4 ozs......................... 93

canned, 4 ozs. with liquid........................... 59

fried, 1 25

littleneck, raw, 6 55

steamed, 3 with a little butter 75

Cocoa,

½ cup 84

Hershey's, powder, 1 T............................. 20

Coconut,

fresh, 1 piece, 1″ x 1″ x ½″ 80

shredded, 1 T...................................... 42

fresh, shredded, ¼ cup 85

dried, sweetened, shredded, ¼ cup.................... 85

Coconut milk (liquid from coconut), ½ cup.............. 27

Cod,

broiled with butter, 2 ozs............................ 97

canned, 4 ozs. 97

dried, salted, 2 ozs................................. 74

frozen fillets (Bird's Eye), 2 fillets, 4 ozs.............. 84
frozen fish sticks (Bird's Eye), 2 sticks 100

Coffee,
prepared, plain, 1 cup 2
with 1 T. milk 10
instant, prepared plain, 1 cup 3

Collards,
raw, ½ lb.. 70
boiled in water, drained, ½ cup...................... 33
frozen greens (Bird's Eye), ½ cup.................... 44

Condiments, see individual listings

Cookies, 1
almond (Keebler Jan Hagel) 47
animal crackers,
   Barnum's 12
   Keebler 8
   Sunshine... 10
anise flavored,
   Stella D'Oro Anisette Sponge 50
   Stella D'Oro Anisette Toast....................... 34
apple flavored,
   Keebler Dutch Apple.............................. 34
   Nabisco Apple Strudel............................ 48
applesauce, Sunshine................................. 33
arrowroot,
   Nabisco National 22
   Sunshine... 15
brown edge, Nabisco Wafers.......................... 28
brownie bar, Nabisco................................. 55
brown sugar, Nabisco Family Favorite................. 25
butter flavored,
   Keebler Old-Fashioned............................ 84
   Nabisco.. 37
   Pepperidge Farm Bordeaux 38

Keebler 23

Nabisco. 30

Sunshine, large. 32

Sunshine, small 17

graham crackers,

    Keebler Honey 17

    Keebler Thin. 17

    Keebler Very Thin 14

    Nabisco. 30

    Sunshine. 17

    Sunshine Sugar Honey. 30

    chocolate covered, Keebler Deluxe 44

    chocolate covered, Nabisco 55

Hermits, 3″ dia. 48

ice box cookies, 2″ dia. 47

iced home-made cookie 100

lady finger 37

lemon, Keebler Old-Fashioned 83

lemon snap, Nabisco 17

lemon-nut, Pepperidge Farm Crunch. 58

macaroons,

    sandwich, Nabisco. 71

    Sunshine. 85

    butter flavored, Sunshine 39

Mallomar 60

Mallo Puffs. 70

marshmallow,

    chocolate covered, Keebler Chocolate Dainties 68

    Keebler Chocolate Treasures 83

    Keebler Galaxies 82

    Keebler Tulips 83

    Nabisco Puffs. 94

    iced, Sunshine Frosted Cakes 68

    iced, Sunshine Nut Sundae 74

    sandwich, Nabisco. 32

sandwich, Keebler 81

molasses, 3" dia. 50

oatmeal,

    homemade, 2" in diameter........................ 75

    Keebler Old-Fashioned........................... 78

    Nabisco Family Favorite.......................... 24

    Nabisco Home Style 61

    Sunshine....................................... 60

    iced, Keebler 82

    w/ whole raisins, Pepperidge Farm.................. 54

orange thins 50

peanuts, Sunshine 33

peanut butter patties, Sunshine 30

peanut creme patties, Nabisco....................... 34

peanut butter, Sunshine 68

pecan,

    Keebler Krisp.................................. 20

    Sunshine Crunch 78

raisin.. 34

raisin, Sunshine Golden Fruit 73

raisin, iced, Keebler Bars 81

shortbread,

    Keebler 27

    Lorna Doone 38

    Scottie.. 39

    cashew, Nabisco................................ 50

    chocolate covered, Nabisco 50

    coconut, iced, Keebler.......................... 65

    iced, Keebler Fudge Stripes....................... 58

    pecan, Keebler Sandies 84

    Nabisco.. 77

Social Tea.. 21

sour cream, 2¼" dia. 56

spiced wafer, Nabisco 33

sugar.. 64

sugar, Keebler Giant 70

sugar, Keebler Old-Fashioned 81

sugar, Nabisco Snaps............................... 17

sugar wafers,

    Keebler, 14 oz. pkg. all flavors..................... 31

    Keebler, 7 oz. pkg. chocolate 26

    Keebler, 7 oz. pkg. strawberry 25

    Keebler, 7 oz. pkg. vanilla 25

    Nabisco.. 18

    Sunshine....................................... 47

    chocolate covered, Nabisco 76

    chocolate covered, Nabisco Creme Stix 50

    chocolate covered, Sunshine ice box................. 30

    spiced, Nabisco 33

vanilla,

    Keebler Wafers.................................. 19

    Nabisco Snaps 13

    Nabisco Wafers 18

    Sunshine Wafers................................. 14

    waffle creme, Nabisco............................ 47

Corn,

    boiled, drained, on cob, 1 ear, 5″ x 1¾″................ 71

    boiled, drained, kernels, ½ cup 69

    canned, cream style, ½ cup......................... 94

    canned, whole kernels, drained, ½ cup 70

    frozen, cream style (Bird's Eye), ½ cup................ 85

    frozen, kernels, ½ cup............................. 77

    frozen, on cob (Bird's Eye), 1 ear.................... 82

    frozen, with butter sauce (Bird's Eye), ½ cup 100

    frozen, with peas and tomatoes (Bird's Eye), ½ cup 71

    frozen, with carrots and pearl onions in cream sauce, ¼ cup   60

Corn fritter, 1 95

Corn grits, cooked, ½ cup 62

Corn meal, cooked, ½ cup 59

Corn muffin, see Muffins

Cornstarch, 1 T.   29

Cowpeas,
    boiled, drained, ½ cup   86
    canned, ½ cup with liquid.   70

Crab,
    fresh, steamed, meat only, 2 ozs.   53
    canned, drained, 2 ozs.   58
    canned, drained, ½ cup   86

Crab apples, 1   30

Cracker meal, 1 T.   43

Crackers, (1 piece)
    bacon flavored, thin (Nabisco)   11
    barbecue snack.   17
    butter.   20
    Cheese-Nips   5
    cheese sandwich.   44
    Cheese Tid-Bits   4
    Cheez-it   6
    Chicken-in-a-Biskit   10
    Chippers   14
    Dutch Rusk   61
    Hi-Ho   17
    Holland Rusk   38
    Krispy.   12
    Matzos, 6″ piece   78
    Matzos, ½ sheet as packaged:
        Manischewitz Regular   60
        Manischewitz Egg   68
        Manischewitz Egg and Onion   66
        Manischewitz Thin Teas   55
        Manischewitz Whole Wheat   63
    Meal-Mates.   22

Melba toast,

    white, regular (Old London) 16

    white, round (Old London) 8

    rounds, garlic flavored (Old London) 9

    wheat (Old London)............................... 16

Oatmeal,... 39

Oyster (Keebler)................................... 3

Oysterettes 3

Oyster (Sunshine).................................. 4

Ritz.. 18

Ritz cheese.. 18

Ry-krisp, 1 double square 20

Rye wafer 25

Saltines,

    Premium 12

    Keebler salt-free 14

    Keebler 14

    Krispy.. 12

Sociables 10

Soda 26

Triangle Thins 8

Triscuits 22

Uneeda 22

wheat or rye thins 10

Zwieback (Nabisco)................................ 31

Cranberries,

    1 cup.. 54

    fresh, ½ lb..................................... 100

Cranberry juice cocktail, canned, 4 ozs. 82

Cranberry Sauce,

    jellied, canned (Ocean Spray), 1 oz.................. 46

    canned, sweetened, 1 T.......................... 25

    whole, canned (Ocean Spray) 1 oz. 48

Cream,

    light or table, 1 T. 32

half and half, ¼ cup 81

half and half, 1 T. 20

half and half, sour (Borden's), ¼ cup................... 81

sour (Borden's), 1 T. 29

sour (Foremost), 1 T. 31

whipping light, 1 T. unwhipped 45

whipping, heavy, 1 T. unwhipped..................... 53

Cream puff, ½ 100

Cream substitutes (non-dairy),

half and half (Meadow Gold), 1 T..................... 27

half and half (Reddi-Whip Coffee White), 1 T............. 21

Coffee Mate, 1 T................................... 33

Cremora, 1 T...................................... 33

Croquettes,

beef, ½ med....................................... 100

chicken, ½ med 88

fish, ½ med 63

potato, ½ med 86

Croutons, ½" cube 5

Cucumber,

fresh, ½ lb.. 33

fresh, peeled, 1 average 7½" x 2" 29

fresh, peeled, 6 slices, 2" x ⅛" 7

Currants,

black, fresh, 1 cup 60

black, cooked, swt., ½ cup.......................... 60

red or white, fresh, ¼ lb. 55

Custard, see Pudding and Pie fillings.

Dandelion greens, raw, ¼ lb. 51

Dandelion greens, boiled, drained, ½ cup 30

Dates, natural and dry, 1 average 22

Dessert topping,

aerosol, 1 T....................................... 10

frozen, 1 T.. 16

mix, prepared, 1 T. 10

Deviled meats,

    ham (Armour Star), 1 T. 40

    ham (Underwood), 1 T. 45

Dextromaltose, 1 T. 40

Donuts,

    ½ plain 68

    cruller, sugared, ½ 80

    jelly, ½ 88

    sugared or iced, ½ 75

Dips,

    bacon and horseradish (Kraft), ½ oz. 36

    blue cheese (Kraft), ½ oz............................. 35

    clam (Kraft), ½ oz. 34

    dill pickle (Kraft), ½ oz............................. 34

    onion (Kraft), ½ oz.................................. 34

Duck, roasted, 1 small slice 100

Eel, smoked, 1 oz....................................... 95

Eggs (chicken),

    raw, whole, 1 large 80

    raw, whole, 1 med. 77

    raw, whole, 1 small 75

    raw, white of 1 large 18

    raw, white of 1 med. 17

    raw, white of 1 small 16

    raw, yolk of 1 large 62

    raw, yolk of 1 med. 60

    raw, yolk of 1 small 59

    boiled, 1 large 80

    boiled, 1 med. 77

    boiled, 1 small 75

    deviled, ½ 80

    fried, with minimum of butter or margarine, 1 100

poached, 1 large...................................... 80

poached, 1 med....................................... 77

poached, 1 small 75

scrambled in teflon pan with no butter,
     oil or margarine.................... same as raw listing

dried, whole, 1 T. 42

Eggnog,

6% fat (Borden's), ¼ cup............................ 81

8% fat (Borden's), ¼ cup............................ 93

Eggplant, boiled, drained, diced, ½ cup 19

Eggroll,

½ of roll 90

frozen (Chun King), 1 roll as packaged 46

frozen (Chun King Party Pack), 1 roll as packaged 23

shrimp, frozen (Chun King), 1 roll as packaged........... 53

Elderberries, fresh, ¼ lb. 77

Enchilada, beef, frozen (Banquet), ½ of one as packaged..... 94

Endive,

raw, ½ lb... 40

raw, 10 small leaves................................ 5

Escarole,

raw, ½ lb... 40

raw, 4 large leaves 20

raw, 7 small leaves................................ 4

Fennel leaves, raw ½ lb. 58

Figs,

fresh, ¼ lb....................................... 81

fresh, 1 small, 1½" dia. 30

candied, 1 oz....................................... 85

canned, 3 figs with 2 T. heavy syrup.................. 96

dried, 1 large, 2" x 1"............................. 57

Filberts,

10 to 12 nuts...................................... 95

1 nut, approximately 8

Finnan haddie, 2 ozs. 59

Fish, see individual listings

Fish cakes, fried, frozen, 1 oz. 77

Fish flakes, canned, 2 ozs. 63

Fish sticks,

    frozen, 2 ozs. 100

    see also Cod and Haddock

Flounder, fresh or frozen, baked with 2 tsp. butter, 1 oz. 56

Frankfurters,

    cooked, 1 oz. 86

    cooked, ½ average 76

    canned, 1 oz. 63

Frog leg, fried 70

Fruit, see individual listings

Fruit juice, mixed,

    bottled, apple and apricot (Mott's), ¼ cup 52

    bottled, apple and cherry (Mott's), ¼ cup 55

    bottled, apple and pineapple (Mott's), ¼ cup 64

    bottled, apple and raspberry (Mott's), ¼ cup 56

    bottled, apple and strawberry (Mott's), ¼ cup 52

Fruit cocktail,

    canned, heavy syrup, ½ cup with liquid 97

    canned, water pack, ½ cup with liquid 44

Fruit drink, canned (Mott's A.M.,P.M.), 2 ozs. 68

Fruit punch, canned (Hi-C), 4 ozs. 65

Fruit salad, bottled (Kraft), 4 ozs. 68

Garlic,

    raw, 1 oz. 39

    raw, 1 average clove 3

Gefilte fish, 4 ozs. 75

Gelatin, unflavored, dry (Knox), 1 envelope 28

Gelatin dessert, all flavors, prepared (Jell-O), ½ cup 81

Gelatin, (D-Zerta), 1 serving (2 servings per pkg.)   12

Gelatin drink, cranberry or orange, dry (Knox), 1 envelope . . .   79

Ginger root,
    fresh, 1 oz.   14
    candied, 1 oz.   96

Goose, roasted, meat only, no skin, 1 oz.   67

Gooseberries,
    fresh, ½ lb.   88
    canned, heavy syrup, ¼ cup with liquid.   54
    canned, water pack, ½ cup with liquid.   31

Granadilla, see Passionfruit

Grape drink, canned (Welchade), 6 ozs.   90

Grape juice,
    canned, or bottled, 4 ozs.   84
    frozen, sweetened, diluted, 4 ozs   66

Grape juice drink, canned or bottled, 4 ozs.   67

Grapes,
    American type (Concord, Delaware, etc.), 22 to 24 grapes .   78
    European type (Halaga, Muscovy, Tokay, Thompson seed-
       less), 22 to 24 grapes.   74
    canned, water pack, ½ cup with liquid.   51

Grapefruit,
    pink, fresh, ½ average, 4½″ dia.   58
    pink, fresh, sections, ½ cup   39
    white, fresh, seeded, ½ average, 4½″ dia.   52
    white, fresh, seedless, ½ average, 4½″ dia.   53
    white, fresh, sections, ½ cup   38
    canned, syrup pack, ½ cup with liquid   87
    canned, water pack, ½ cup with liquid.   36

Grapefruit juice,
    fresh, 8 ozs.   96
    canned, sweetened, 4 ozs.   67
    canned, unsweetened, 4 ozs.   51

frozen, sweetened, diluted, 4 ozs. 59

frozen, unsweetened, diluted, 4 ozs. 51

Grapefruit-orange juice,

canned, sweetened, 4 ozs............................ 63

canned, unsweetened, 4 ozs.......................... 53

frozen, unsweetened, diluted, 4 ozs. 55

Grapefruit peel,

candied, 1 oz...................................... 90

grated, 1 T.. 32

Gravy,

beef,

canned (Franco-American), ¼ cup 30

canned (Ready Gravy), ¼ cup....................... 42

brown (Howard Johnson's), ¼ cup 40

mix, prepared as on pkg. (Wyler's), ¼ cup 24

(Durkee) ¼ cup 18

(French's) ¼ cup 18

(McCormick) ¼ cup........................... 29

chicken,

canned (College Inn), ¼ cup....................... 24

canned (Franco-American), ¼ cup 53

mix, (Durkee), ¼ cup 26

mix, (French's), ¼ cup 31

mix, (McCormick), ¼ cup......................... 24

mix, (Wyler's), ¼ cup 24

chicken giblet, canned (Franco-American), ¼ cup........ 28

herb mix, (McCormick), ¼ cup 26

mushroom,

canned (Franco-American), ¼ cup 30

mix, (Durkee), ¼ cup 24

mix, (French's), ¼ cup 16

mix, (McCormick), ¼ cup......................... 20

mix, (Wyler's), ¼ cup 15

onion,

mix, (Durkee), ¼ cup 28

mix, (French's), ¼ cup 18

mix, (McCormick), ¼ cup......................... 30

mix, (Wyler's), ¼ cup 17

turkey giblet, canned (Howard Johnson's), ¼ cup 40

Grouper, raw, flesh only, 4 ozs. 99

Guavas, fresh, 1 small 48

Guinea hen, ¾ oz...................................... 78

Gum, chewing (1 stick),

Beechnut... 10

Chiclets... 5

Dentyne 5

Doublemint.. 8

Juicy Fruit 8

Wrigley's Spearmint................................ 8

Haddock,

frozen (Bird's Eye), 4 ozs. 88

frozen, fish sticks (Bird's Eye), 1 stick................. 70

smoked, 2 ozs..................................... 59

Halibut,

fresh or frozen, broiled with 1 tsp. butter, 2 ozs........... 94

smoked, 1 oz...................................... 64

Ham,

boiled, 1 oz....................................... 67

fresh, med. fat, roasted, ½ oz. 53

light cure, med. fat, roasted, 1 oz. 83

light cure, lean only, roasted, 1 oz. 53

long cure, country style, med. fat, ½ oz................ 59

long cure, country style, lean only, ½ oz. 44

minced, 1 oz....................................... 65

picnic, cured, med. fat, roasted, 1 oz. 92

picnic, cured, lean only, roasted, 1 oz.................. 60

canned, deviled, 1 oz. 100

Prosciutto, ¾ oz. 85

Hamburger, see Beef, ground

Hash, canned, see Beef, corned

Hazelnuts, 10 to 12 nuts 95

Heart,
    beef, braised, 1 oz. 54
    calf, braised, 1 oz................................... 59
    chicken, simmered, 2 ozs. 99

Herbs 0

Herring,
    raw Atlantic, 2 ozs................................. 100
    raw Pacific, 2 ozs.................................. 56
    canned, plain, 1 oz. with liquid 59
    canned in tomato sauce, 2 ozs. with liquid 100
    pickled, Bismarck-type, 1 oz......................... 63
    salted or brined, 1 oz. 62
    smoked, bloaters, 1 oz. 56
    smoked, bard, 1 oz................................. 85
    smoked, kippered, 1 oz. 60

Hickory nuts, 1 nut 7

Hollandaise sauce,
    in jars (Lord Mott's), ¼ cup 57
    see also Sauce, mix

Hominy grits, cooked, ½ cup 82

Honey, strained or extracted,
    1 oz... 86
    1 T.. 64

Honeydew melon, fresh,
    ½ lb... 47
    1 wedge, 2" x 7"................................. 49
    ½ cup diced 40

Horseradish,
    prepared, 1 T...................................... 8
    raw, 1 oz. 18

Huckleberries, 1 cup 85

Ice bar, all flavors,

    Eskimo Twin Pop, 1 bar as pkgd...................... 24

    Popsicle, 3 fl. ozs. bar 70

    Kool Pops, 1 bar as pkgd........................... 27

Ice cream,

    all flavors, mix, prepared (Junket Freezing mix), ⅙ pt. 78

    chocolate

        Sealtest, ⅙ pint 96

        Borden's, ⅙ pint 86

        Meadowgold, ⅙ pint 86

    strawberry

        Sealtest, ⅙ pint 87

        Borden's, ⅙ pint 84

        Meadowgold, ⅙ pint 84

    vanilla

        Sealtest, ⅙ pint 88

        Borden's, ⅙ pint 88

        Lady Borden, ⅙ pint 100

        Meadowgold, ⅙ pint 84

    vanilla-chocolate, Sealtest Checkerboard, ⅙ pint.......... 90

    vanilla-fudge, Sealtest Royale, ⅙ pint 91

Ice cream bar,

    chocolate coating

        Sealtest, ½ of a 3-oz. bar 81

        Eskimo Pie, ½ bar.............................. 100

    vanilla, sherbet coated (Creamsicle), 3-oz. bar 96

Ice cream patty, mint flavored, chocolate coated, (Eskimo Pie Thin Mint), ½ patty................................. 64

Ice cream sandwich,

    Sealtest, ⅓ of a sandwich 69

    vanilla, chocolate coated (Eskimo), ½ sandwich 62

Ice cream cone,

    sugar (Comet), 1 cone 37

    waffle (Nabisco), 1 cone 19

Ice milk,
  vanilla,
    Sealtest, ⅙ pint 68
    Borden's, ⅙ pint 76
    Meadowgold, ⅙ pint 63
    Lady Borden, ⅙ pint 82

Ice milk bar, chocolate coated (Sealtest), ½ bar 72

Ices made with milk, ⅛ pint 71

Ices made with water, ⅛ pint 59

Ices, orange (Sealtest), ⅙ pint 71

Jams and preserves, all flavors,
  1 oz. 77
  1 T. 54

Jellies, all flavors,
  1 oz. 78
  1 T. 55

Juices, see individual listings

Kale,
  raw, ½ lb. 77
  boiled, drained, ½ cup 15
  frozen, chopped (Bird's Eye), ½ cup 29

Kidneys,
  beef or veal, 2 ozs. 80
  lamb, 3 ozs. 89
  pork, 3 ozs. 97

Kingfish, raw, flesh only, 2 ozs. 60

Knockwurst, 1 oz. 79

Kohlrabi,
  raw, without leaves, ½ lb. 48
  boiled, drained, ½ cup 19

Kumquats,
  fresh, ¼ lb. 69
  fresh, 4 average 39

Lamb, choice grade cuts,

    chop, loin, lean and fat, broiled, 1 oz. with bone 100

    chop, loin, lean only, broiled, 2¼ ozs.................. 70

    leg, lean and fat, roasted, 1 oz......................... 80

    leg, lean only, roasted, 1 oz........................... 53

    shoulder, lean and fat, roasted, 1 oz. 96

    shoulder, lean only, roasted, 1 oz...................... 59

Leeks,

    raw, ½ lb... 62

    1 average... 17

    2 stalks, 5″ long.................................... 24

Lemonade,

    frozen, diluted, 1 cup............................... 75

    pink, frozen, diluted (Bird's Eye), 6 ozs................ 77

    mix, (Wyler's), 8 ozs. 81

    made with 1 oz. lemon juice and 2 T. sugar, 8 ozs. 100

Lemon juice,

    fresh, ½ cup 30

    fresh, 1 T.. 4

    canned or bottled, unsweetened, ½ cup 28

    canned or bottled, unsweetened, 1 T. 3

    frozen, unsweetened, diluted, ½ cup 26

    frozen, unsweetened, diluted, 1 T. 3

    frozen, unsweetened, undiluted concentrate, 1 T........... 17

Lemon peel,

    candied, 1 oz....................................... 90

    candied, grated, 1 T. 32

Lemons,

    fresh, ½ lb... 45

    fresh, 1 average, 2¼″ dia. 20

Lentils, whole, cooked, ¼ cup 51

Lettuce,

    Boston or Bib, ¼ lb.................................. 24

    Boston or Bib, 1 head, 4″ dia. 31

iceberg, ½ lb.. 28

iceberg, 1 head, 4¾″ dia. 59

iceberg, 3 average leaves............................. 6

romaine, ½ lb... 26

romaine, 3 leaves, 8″ long............................ 5

Simpson or looseleaf, ½ lb. 26

Simpson or looseleaf, 2 large leaves.................. 9

Lichee nuts,

raw, ¼ lb... 44

dried, 6 nuts... 41

1 nut 7

Lime juice,

fresh, ½ cup.. 32

fresh, 1 T.. 4

canned or bottled, unsweetened, ½ cup 32

canned or bottled, unsweetened, 1 T. 4

Limeade, frozen, diluted, 6 ozs........................ 77

Limes,

fresh, ½ lb... 54

fresh, 1 average, 1½″ long 19

Liver,

beef, fried, 1 oz. 65

calf, fried, 1 oz..................................... 74

chicken, simmered, 1 oz. 47

hog, fried, 1 oz...................................... 69

lamb, broiled, 1 oz................................... 75

turkey, simmered, 1 oz................................ 49

Liver spread, 1 T...................................... 95

Liverwurst,

fresh, 1 oz... 88

smoked, 1 oz.. 91

Lobster,

canned or cooked, meat only, 2 ozs. 54

creamed, ¼ cup 75

Lobster paste, 1 oz. 51

Loganberries,
    fresh, ¼ lb.. 67
    fresh, ½ cup 45

Loquats, fresh, ½ lb.................................. 84

Lox, 3 ozs.. 81

Luncheon meat, see also individual listings
    boiled ham, 1 oz. slice 85
    spiced ham, canned, 1 oz. slice 80
    ham and cheese (Oscar Mayer), 1 slice................. 76

Macadamia nuts, 6 nuts............................... 90

Macaroni,
    boiled 8-10 minutes, drained, ½ cup 96
    boiled 14-20 minutes, drained, ½ cup 78
    canned, creole (Heinz), 4 ozs. 74
    canned, with cheese, 3 ozs. 81

Mackerel,
    fresh or frozen, broiled with 2 tsp. butter, 1 oz. 66
    canned Atlantic, 1 oz. with liquid.................... 52
    canned Pacific, 1 oz. with liquid..................... 51
    salted, 1 oz. 87
    smoked, 1 oz...................................... 63

Malted milk powder, 1 T. 50

Mangoes,
    fresh, ¼ lb.. 51
    fresh, ½ average, 3¾" long........................ 67

Margarine,
    diet or imitation, 1 T.............................. 50
    salted or unsalted, ½ T............................ 51
    salted or unsalted, 1 pat (16 per ¼ lb.)................. 51

Marmalade, citrus flavors,
    1 oz. 73
    1 T. 51

Mayonnaise, see Salad dressings

Meat, see individual listings

Melon balls,
frozen (Bird's Eye), ¼ package, 4 ozs. 36
frozen in syrup, 4 ozs............................... 70

Milk, cow's,
evaporated, ¼ cup 87
whole, 3.5% fat, ½ cup.............................. 80
whole, 3.7% fat, ½ cup.............................. 81
buttermilk, cultured, 8 ozs........................... 89
chocolate, commercial, ½ cup........................ 93
skim milk, 8 ozs.................................... 89
dry, nonfat, instant, 1 T. 26

Milk, goat's, whole, 4 ozs............................. 82

Milk, malted,
chocolate (Borden's), powder, 1 heaping tsp............. 39
natural (Borden's), powder, 1 heaping tsp. 40

Mint, chopped, 1 T.................................... 1

Molasses, see Syrups

Muffins,
blueberry, ½ small 63
bran, ½ medium.................................... 53
corn (Thomas's), ½ muffin 90
corn, mix, prepared as on pkg. (Dromedary), ½ muffin 96
date, mix, prepared as on pkg. (Dromedary), ½ muffin 92
egg, ½ medium muffin 63
English (Thomas's), ½ muffin........................ 70
raisin, ½ medium muffin............................. 65
rye, ½ medium muffin............................... 68
white, ½ medium muffin............................. 60
whole wheat, ½ medium muffin....................... 60

Mushrooms,
raw, ½ lb.. 61

4 large   10

canned, 4 ozs. with liquid.   19

Mussels, canned, drained, 2 ozs.   65

Mustard greens,

raw, ½ lb.   49

boiled, drained, ½ cup   16

frozen, ½ cup.   19

Mustard spinach,

raw, ½ lb.   50

boiled, drained, ½ cup   14

Mustard,

prepared, brown, 1 oz.   26

prepared, yellow, 1 oz.   21

Nectarines,

fresh, ¼ lb.   67

fresh, 1 average   30

Noodles, egg, cooked, ½ cup. 100

Noodles, prepared as directed on pkg.,

Noodle-Roni Casserole, ½ cup   96

Noodle-Roni Parmesano, ¼ cup   64

Noodle-Roni Romanoff, ¼ cup   91

Noodles, with beef, canned (Heinz Minute Meal), ½ of an 8-oz.

can   66

Noodles with beef,

in gravy, in jars (College Inn), ⅓ cup   79

in tomato sauce, in jars (College Inn), ⅓ cup   79

Noodles with chicken, in jars (College Inn), ½ cup   83

Nuts, see individual listings

Oats, Oatmeal, see Cereals

Oil,

cod liver, 1 T. 100

corn (Mazola), ½ T. . . . .   60 cottonseed (Kraft), winterized, ½ T.   64

halibut liver, 1 T.   100

olive, ½ T.   63

peanut, ½ T.   62

safflower (Kraft), ½ T.   64

salad or cooking, ½ T.   62

soybean, ½ T.   63

Okra,

raw, ½ lb.   70

boiled, drained, 8 pods, 3″ long   25

frozen (Bird's Eye), ½ cup   36

Oleomargarine, see Margarine

Olives, pickled, canned or bottled,

green, 4 medium or 3 large   15

ripe, Mission, 3 small or 2 large   15

Onion rings, French fried, frozen,

(Bird's Eye), 2 ozs.   73

(Mrs. Paul's), ½ of a 5 oz. pkg.   100

Onions,

mature, ½ lb.   79

raw, average 2¼″ dia.   40

raw, chopped, 1 T.   4

boiled, drained, ½ cup   30

dehydrated flakes, 1 oz.   99

Onions, green

raw, bulb and entire top, ½ lb.   79

raw, bulb and white part, ½ lb.   38

raw, bulb and white part, 3 small   11

Onions, sour, pickled (Heinz), 2 average   1

Orange-apricot juice drink, canned, 6 ozs.   93

Ornage-grapefruit juice, see Grapefruit-orange juice

Orange drink, canned (Hi-C), 6 ozs.   88

Orange juice,

Calif. navel, fresh, 6 ozs. 90

Calif. Valencia, fresh, 6 ozs. 88

Fla. early and midseason, fresh, 8 ozs. 99

Fla. Valencia, fresh, 6 ozs. 84

canned, sweetened, 6 ozs. 97

canned, unsweetened, 6 ozs. 90

dehydrated crystals with water, 6 ozs. 85

frozen, diluted, 6 ozs. 84

frozen, reconstituted, (Bird's Eye), 6 ozs. 72

frozen, reconstituted, (Minute Maid), 6 ozs. 90

frozen, reconstituted, (Snow Crop), 6 ozs. 90

Orange juice drink,

powder with water (Tang), 6 ozs. 89

frozen, diluted (Awake), 6 ozs. 93

Orange peel,

candied, 1 oz. 90

candied, grated, 1 T. 32

Orange-pineapple drink, canned (Hi-C), 6 ozs. 88

Oranges,

canned, mandarin, ⅓ cup 55

Fla., all varieties, fresh ½ lb. 79

Fla., all varieties, fresh, 1 average, 3″ dia. 75

Navel, fresh, ½ lb. 79

Navel, fresh, 1 average, 3″ dia. 61

sections, fresh, ½ cup 47

Ovaltine with milk, ⅓ cup 74

Oysters,

Eastern, raw, meat only, 4 ozs. 75

fried, 1 50

Pacific or Western, raw, meat only, 3 ozs. 77

Rockefeller, 3 93

canned, 4 ozs. with liquid. 86

Oyster stew with milk, ½ cup........................... 100

Oyster stew made with skim milk, ½ cup 78

Pancakes, mix, prepared as directed on package,
    regular (Aunt Jemima), 4″ dia. 61
    buckwheat (Aunt Jemima), 4″ dia. 64
    buttermilk (Aunt Jemima), 4″ dia. 71

Papaya juice, canned, 6 ozs............................ 90

Papayas,
    fresh, ½ lb... 60
    fresh, ½ cup of ½″ cubes............................ 36

Paprika, ⅛ tsp.. 0

Parsely, raw, chopped, 1 T. 2

Parsnips, boiled, drained, ½ cup 51

Passionfruit, fresh, ¼ lb.............................. 53

Pastrami, 1 oz.. 85

Pâté de foie gras, canned, ½ oz........................ 85

Peach nectar, canned, 6 ozs............................ 90

Peaches,
    fresh, 1 average, 2″ dia............................ 35
    fresh, sliced, ½ cup............................... 33
    candied, 1 oz...................................... 90
    canned, heavy syrup, ½ cup with liquid.............. 100
    canned, 2 medium halves with 2 T. heavy syrup......... 88
    canned, spiced (Hunts), ½.......................... 88
    canned, water pack, ½ cup with liquid............... 38
    dried, cooked, sweetened, ¼ cup with liquid........... 95
    dried, cooked, unsweetened, ¼ cup with liquid......... 56
    frozen, sweetened, sliced, ¼ cup 55

Peanut butter,
    (Skippy), 1 T...................................... 100
    (Planters), 1 T.................................... 100
    (Jif), 1 T... 72

Peanuts,

    1 nut 5

    roasted and salted, chopped, 1 T. 54

    Spanish, 10 nuts. 50

Pear nectar, canned, 6 ozs. 99

Pears,

    fresh, 1 average, 2½″ dia. 100

    candied, 1 oz. 86

    canned, heavy syrup, ½ cup with liquid. 97

    canned, 2 medium halves with 2 T. heavy syrup. 89

    canned, water pack, ½ cup with liquid. 39

Peas, black-eye,

    canned, ½ cup with liquid. 70

    frozen, ½ cup. 92

Peas, green,

    boiled, drained, ½ cup 57

    canned, ½ cup with liquid. 82

    canned, drained, ½ cup. 70

    frozen, ½ cup. 69

    frozen, with butter sauce (Bird's Eye), ½ cup 97

    frozen, with celery (Bird's Eye), ½ cup 58

    frozen, with cream sauce (Bird's Eye), ½ cup 69

    frozen, with mushrooms (Bird's Eye), ½ cup. 66

Peas, split, boiled, drained, ¼ cup. 58

Peas and carrots, frozen, ½ cup 52

Pecans,

    half of 1 9

    chopped, 1 T. 51

Peppers, hot chili,

    raw, green, ½ lb. 62

    red, raw, ¼ lb. 54

    dried, ground, see Chili powder

Peppers, sweet, green

    raw, ½ lb. 41

    raw, seeded, 1 average 14

    raw, seeded, diced, ½ cup 10

    boiled, drained, seeded, 1 average 11

Peppers, sweet, raw, red,

    ½ lb. 56

    1 average. 19

Perch,

    ocean, fresh or frozen, 2 ozs. baked with 1 tsp. butter 80

    white, raw, 1 fillet, 3 ozs. 100

    frozen fillets (Bird's Eye), 2 fillets, 4 ozs. 100

Persian melon, 1 wedge 52

Persimmons, Japanese or kaki, seedless, fresh, 1 average 81

Pickle relish:

    barbecue (Heinz), 1 T. 32

    hamburger (Heinz), 1 T. 17

    sour, 1 oz. 8

    sour, 1 T. 2

    sweet, 1 oz. 39

    sweet, 1 T. 18

Pickles,

    dill, 4 ozs. 12

    dill, 1 large, 4″ x 1¾″ 15

    mixed, chopped, 1 T. 14

    sour, 4 ozs. 11

    sour, 1 large, 4″ x 1¾″ 14

    sweet, 1 average, 2¾″ x ¾″ 29

Pie crust, bottom only, ¹⁄₁₆ of a 9″ dia. crust 41

Pig's feet,

    boiled, 2 ozs. 93

    pickled, 1 oz. 57

Pike, raw,

    blue, flesh only, 3 ozs. 77

northern, flesh only, 4 ozs. 100

wall-eye, flesh only, 3 ozs. 78

Pimientos, canned, 1 average 10

Pineapple,

fresh, ½ lb. 62

1 slice, fresh, 3½" x ¾". 44

fresh, diced, ½ cup 36

candied, 1 oz. 90

canned, heavy syrup, chunks, ½ cup with liquid. 85

canned, heavy syrup, crushed, ½ cup with liquid 96

canned, 1 large slice with 2 T. heavy syrup. 90

frozen, sweetened, chunks, ½ cup 100

Pineapple juice,

canned, unsweetened, 4 ozs. 69

frozen, unsweetened, diluted, 4 ozs. 65

Pineapple-grapefruit juice drink, 4 ozs. 67

Pineapple-orange juice drink, canned, 4 ozs. 67

Pistachio nuts,

1 nut, ...   3

1 T. chopped. 53

Pizza, cheese, ⅟₁₆ of a 14" pie 93

Plums,

fresh, 1 average, 2" dia. 36

prune-type, fresh, 1 average 24

canned, purple, 2 plums with 1 T. heavy syrup. 65

Pomegranates, fresh, ½ lb. 80

Pompano, raw, flesh only, 2 ozs. 94

Popcorn,

plain, 1 cup 54

candied, ½ cup. 50

Popover, 1. 90

Popsicle, see Ice bars

Pork,

    Boston butt, lean and fat, roasted, 1 oz.................. 100

    Boston butt, lean only, roasted, 1 oz.................... 70

    chop, very small and thin 100

    loin, lean and fat, roasted, 1 oz....................... 100

    loin, lean only, roasted, 1 oz. 73

    spareribs, 2 medium 41

Pork and beans, see Beans, baked

Pork and gravy, canned, 1 oz........................... 73

Pork sausage, see Sausages

Postum, 1 cup.. 36

Potato chips, 8 chips, 2″ dia. 96

Potato pancake, ½ 55

Potato sticks (Wise Julienne), ½ oz...................... 69

Potatoes, white,

    baked, including skin, 1 small 93

    boiled in skin, 1 small.............................. 76

    boiled, peeled, 1 small.............................. 65

    canned, 4 ozs. with liquid........................... 50

    canned, 3 or 4 very small 96

    French fried, 5 pieces, 2″ long 78

    frozen, crinkle-cut (Bird's Eye), 8 pieces 73

    frozen, French fried, heated, 8 pieces 94

    frozen, mashed, heated, ½ cup 93

    frozen patties (Bird's Eye), ½ patty................... 90

    frozen, Tiny Taters (Bird's Eye), scant ¼ pkg. 100

    hash brown, 3 T. 90

    mashed with milk, ½ cup 73

    mashed with milk and butter, ⅓ cup.................. 77

    scalloped, ¼ cup 60

    whipped, mix (Borden's), prepared as directed on pkg. 83

Potatoes, sweet,

    baked, peeled, ½ average, 5″ x 2″ 78

boiled, peeled, ½ average, 5″ x 2″   62

candied, average, ⅓   98

canned, vacuum or solid pack, ¼ cup   55

yams, boiled, drained, diced, ¼ cup   53

Pretzels,

5 small sticks   20

3 small   37

Prune juice, 4 ozs.   99

Prunes,

dried, large size, 1 average   19

dried, medium size, 1 average.   15

dried, small size, 1 average   11

dried, cooked, unsweetened with liquid, ¼ cup.   69

Pudding, Apple Snow, ½ cup   70

Puddings and pie fillings, mix, prepared as directed on package,

Jell-O, all flavors except lemon, ¼ cup   84

banana (Royal), ¼ cup   83

banana custard, ¼ cup.   63

bread pudding, ¼ cup   75

butterscotch (Royal), ¼ cup.   95

caramel, ¼ cup   75

chocolate (Royal), ¼ cup   95

chocolate (Dark 'n' Sweet, Royal), ¼ cup   98

custard (Royal), ¼ cup.   73

Indian, ¼ cup.   75

junket, ¼ cup.   54

lemon (Jell-O), ¼ cup   63

lemon chiffon filling (Jell-O), ¼ cup   72

plum pudding, ½ cup   75

prune whip, ½ cup.   100

Rennet dessert, ¼ cup   65

rice, ¼ cup.   84

tapioca, chocolate (Royal), ¼ cup. . . . .   93 tapioca, vanilla (Royal), ¼ cup 85

vanilla (Royal), ¼ cup 83

Puddings, "instant" mix, prepared as directed on package,

Jell-O, all flavors, ¼ cup........................... 93

banana cream (Royal), ¼ cup 88

butterscotch (Royal), ¼ cup........................ 88

caramel nut (Royal), ¼ cup 98

chocolate (Royal), ¼ cup........................... 100

lemon (Royal), ¼ cup 90

mocha nut (Royal), ¼ cup.......................... 100

vanilla (Royal), ¼ cup 90

Pumpkin, canned, ½ cup................................ 38

Quail, raw, boned, 2 ozs. 86

Quinces, fresh, ¼ lb.................................... 79

Rabbit, domestic, meat only, stewed, 1 oz. 62

Radishes, raw, 1 small................................. 2

Raisins, dried, 1 T. 26

Raspberries,

black, fresh, ½ cup 45

red, fresh, ½ cup 35

canned, water pack, black, with liquid................. 51

canned, water pack, red, with liquid 35

frozen, red (Bird's Eye), ¼ cup...................... 69

Ravioli, cheese filling, 1 square 90

Red snapper, raw, flesh only, 3 ozs..................... 79

Rhubarb, fresh,

1 cup diced....................................... 19

without leaves, ½ lb................................ 31

cooked, sweetened, ¼ cup.......................... 96

frozen (Bird's Eye), ½ cup 84

Rice,

brown, cooked, ½ cup.............................. 100

white, milled, cooked, ½ cup........................ 92

white, parboiled, long grain, cooked, ½ cup............. 89

white, precooked (Minute Rice), ¼ cup 53

Rice mix, prepared as directed on package,

Rice-a-Roni, beef, ¼ cup 80

Rice-a-Roni, chicken, ¼ cup......................... 79

Rice-a-Roni, wild, ¼ cup 71

Rice, Spanish, canned (Heinz), 4 ozs. 61

Rice, wild, ½ cup cooked............................. 68

Rice and peas with mushrooms, frozen (Bird's Eye), ½ cup... 49

Rolls,

hamburger, ½ roll................................. 75

hard, ½ roll 80

frankfurter, ½ roll................................. 80

onion, ½ roll 75

Parker House, ½ roll 63

sweet, ½ roll 89

whole wheat, ½ roll................................ 49

Romaine, see Lettuce

Rutabagas,

raw, without tops, ½ lb. 89

boiled, drained, cubes, ½ cup........................ 35

Salad dressings, commercial,

blue cheese, 1 T. 81

French, 1 T. 62

Italian, 1 T....................................... 83

mayonnaise, ½ T................................... 54

Miracle Whip, 1 T.................................. 70

Roquefort, 1 T..................................... 81

Russian, 1 T. 89

thousand island, 1 T. 75

vinegar and oil, equal parts, 1 T. 63

Salads,

carrot-raisin, 1½ T................................. 75

cole slaw, ½ cup 51

chicken with celery, ¼ cup 100

macaroni, ¼ cup 84

potato with onions, ¼ cup............................. 92

shrimp, with celery, ½ cup 85

tomato aspic, ½ cup................................... 50

tuna, ¼ cup 75

Waldorf, ¼ cup 70

Salami,

cooked, 1 oz... 88

1 slice, ¼" thick...................................... 65

Salmon, fresh or frozen steak,

baked with 1 tsp. butter, 2 ozs....................... 80

broiled with 1 tsp. butter, 1 oz...................... 60

canned, chinook, 1 oz. 60

canned, pink, 2 ozs. 80

canned, red, 2 ozs. 97

smoked, 2 ozs... 100

Sandwich spread,

relish, ½ oz.. 54

1 T... 57

Hellman's, 1 T.. 60

Kraft Miracle, 1 T.................................... 56

Sandwiches. Use individual count for 1 slice bread and whatever filling you use.

Sardines,

canned in brine, Pacific, 1 oz. in liquid.............. 56

canned in mustard, Pacific, 1 oz. with liquid............ 56

canned in oil, Atlantic, drained, 2 ozs. 95

canned in tomato sauce, Pacific, 1 oz. with liquid 57

Sauces, 1 T.,

A-1 15

barbecue.. 17

cheese.. 33

chili.. 18

cocktail.. 25

cream 35

Creole... 25

garlic butter 25

hard... 97

hot pepper... 3

lemon 25

meat, bottled 10

meat, Italian....................................... 12

soy 9

tartar... 74

tomato, canned (Hunt's) 5

white, medium..................................... 27

white, thin 19

Worcestershire 15

Sauces, mix, prepared as directed on package,

cheese (Durkee), ¼ cup............................ 72

Hollandaise (Durkee), ½ cup....................... 59

sour cream, with whole milk (Durkee), ¼ cup 81

sour cream, with skim milk (Durkee), ¼ cup 70

Sauces, sweet, see Syrups and Toppings

Sauerkraut, canned, ½ cup with liquid.................. 21

Sauerkraut juice, 1 cup 40

Sausage, Polish, 1 slice 83

Sausage, pork link,

1 cooked... 95

smoked, country style, 1 oz........................ 98

Sausage patty, ½ cooked 93

Sausage, Vienna, canned, drained, 1 oz. 69

Scallions, see Onions, green

Scallops,

bay or sea, steamed, 2 ozs.......................... 64

breaded, fried, frozen, reheated, 1 oz.   55

Scrapple, 1 oz.   61

Shad,

    fresh, baked with 1 tsp. butter, 1 oz.   56

    fresh, roe, broiled with 1 tsp. butter, 2 ozs.   69

    canned, 2 ozs. with liquid.   86

Sesame seeds, ½ oz.   80

Sherbet, orange,

    Sealtest, ⅙ pt.   76

    Borden's, ⅙ pt.   73

Shortening (Crisco), ½ T.   52

Shrimp,

    fresh, boiled, 4 to 6.   64

    canned, 4 ozs. with liquid.   91

    canned, drained, 2 ozs.   66

    cocktail, 6 with sauce 100

    Creole, 3 with sauce   85

    French fried, dipped in egg, 1 oz.   73

Scampi, 2 in garlic butter   88

Shrimp paste, canned, 1 oz.   51

Smelt, canned, 1 oz. with liquid.   56

Snails, Bourguignonne, 6 100

Soft drinks,

    bitter lemon (Schweppe's), 6 ozs.   96

    bitter orange (Schweppe's), 6 ozs.   93

    cherry soda, 8 ozs.   80

    club soda   0

    cola,

        Coca-Cola, 8 ozs.   96

        Pepsi-Cola, 6 ozs.   78

        Royal Crown, 6 ozs.   83

    cream soda, 6 ozs. . . . .   79 ginger ale,

    Canada Dry, 8 ozs. 85

    Schweppe's, 8 ozs. 88

ginger beer (Schweppe's), 8 ozs. 96

grape soda, 8 ozs. 100

grape soda (Fanta), 6 ozs. 91

Kool-Aid, all flavors, prepared with water and sugar, 8 ozs. 91

lemon-lime, 8 ozs................................... 95

Mountain Dew, 6 ozs............................... 87

orange soda, 8 ozs. 95

quinine water (Schweppe's), 8 ozs.................... 88

root beer,

    Hires, 8 ozs... 96

    Dad's, 6 ozs. 78

    Fanta, 6 ozs....................................... 90

Seven-Up, 8 ozs. 97

soda, seltzer, 8 ozs. 5

Sprite, 8 ozs. 96

Squirt, 8 ozs....................................... 91

strawberry soda (Fanta), 6 ozs. 89

Wink, 6 ozs. 90

Sole, fillets, frozen (Bird's Eye), 2 fillets, 4 ozs. 88

Soup, canned, condensed, diluted with equal amount of water,

barley, ½ cup 59

bean with pork, ¼ cup 84

beef, 1 cup 100

beef bouillon, broth, 1 cup 26

beef, consommé, 1 cup 33

beef noodle, 1 cup 70

bean, ½ cup 96

chicken consommé, 1 cup 23

chicken gumbo, 1 cup 58

chicken noodle, 1 cup 65

chicken vegetable, 1 cup 74

chicken with rice, 1 cup 48

clam chowder, Manhattan, 1 cup..................... 76

fish chowder, ½ cup................................ 100

green pea, ½ cup 65

lentil, ½ cup....................................... 71

lobster bisque, ½ cup............................... 100

onion, 1 cup 45

onion, French, ½ cup 63

pepper pot, 1 cup 100

potato, ½ cup...................................... 93

split pea, ½ cup.................................... 73

tomato, 1 cup 88

turkey noodle, 1 cup 81

vegetable beef, 1 cup............................... 77

vegetable with beef broth, 1 cup..................... 78

vegetarian vegetable, 1 cup 77

Soup, canned, condensed, diluted with equal amount whole milk,

asparagus, cream of, ½ cup.......................... 72

celery, cream of, ½ cup 83

chicken, cream of, ½ cup 87

mushroom, cream of, ¼ cup 53

potato, cream of, ⅓ cup............................. 72

tomato, cream of, ½ cup 83

Soup, frozen, condensed, diluted with equal amount water,

clam chowder, New England, ½ cup 66

green pea with ham, ½ cup.......................... 70

vegetable with beef, 1 cup........................... 86

Soup, frozen, condensed, diluted with equal amount whole milk,

clam chowder, New England, ¼ cup 51

oyster stew, ½ cup 99

potato, cream of, ½ cup............................. 89

shrimp, cream of, ¼ cup 58

Soybeans, boiled, drained, ½ cup....................... 89

Spaghetti,
  boiled 8-10 minutes, drained, ½ cup 96
  boiled 14-20 minutes, drained, ½ cup 78
  with meatballs, ⅓ cup 78
  canned, in tomato sauce with cheese, 4 ozs. 86
  canned, with ground beef (Franco-American), 1 oz. 34
  canned, with hot dogs (Heinz), 2 ozs. 59
  canned, with meatballs in tomato sauce, 2 ozs. 59

Spaghetti sauce, canned,
  with meat (Campbell's), 1 oz. 27
  with mushrooms (Campbell's), 4 ozs. 88

Spinach,
  raw, trimmed, packaged, ½ lb. 59
  boiled, drained, ½ cup 21
  canned, drained, ½ cup 22
  frozen, leaf, ½ cup. 24
  frozen, chopped, ½ cup. 23

Squash, summer,
  scallop variety, boiled, drained, ½ cup. 17
  yellow, boiled, drained, ½ cup 16
  zucchini, boiled, drained, ½ cup 13
  frozen, yellow, ½ cup 13

Squash, winter,
  acorn, baked, mashed, ½ cup 57
  acorn, boiled, mashed, ½ cup. 35
  butternut, baked, mashed, ½ cup 70
  butternut, boiled, mashed, ½ cup. 42
  hubbard, baked, mashed, ½ cup. 52
  hubbard, boiled, mashed, ½ cup. 31
  frozen, cooked, ½ cup. 43

Steak, see Beef

Strawberries,
  fresh, ½ lb. 81

fresh, capped, ½ cup 28

canned, water pack, ½ cup with liquid 29

frozen, halves (Bird's Eye), ¼ cup 78

frozen, whole (Bird's Eye), ½ cup 98

frozen, sweetened, sliced, ¼ lb. can or carton 74

juice, 1 cup 42

Sturgeon,

smoked, 2 ozs. 85

steamed, 2 ozs. 91

Succotash,

frozen, ½ cup 91

canned, ½ cup 75

Sugar,

beet or cane, 1 T. 52

brown, firm, packed, 1 T. 38

corn, 1 T. 60

granulated, 1 T. 46

loaf (4 Dominoes) 100

lump, 1 piece, 1⅛″ x ¾″ x ⅜″ 23

maple, 1″ cube 95

powdered, stirred, 1 T. 31

Sweet potatoes, see Potatoes, sweet

Sweetbreads,

beef, braised, 1 oz. 91

calf, braised, 2 ozs. 96

lamb, braised, 2 ozs. 99

Swordfish,

fresh or frozen, steak, broiled with 1 tsp butter, 2 ozs. 97

canned, 2 ozs. with liquid 58

Syrups,

black raspberry (Kraft), 1 T. 40

blackberry (Kraft), 1 T. 40

butterscotch (Hershey's), 1 T. 55

butterscotch (Kraft), 1 T. 49

butterscotch (Smucker's), 1 T. 48

caramel (Smucker's), 1 T. 48

cherry (Kraft), 1 T. 40

chocolate, thin type, 1 T. 49

chocolate fudge (Hershey's), 1 T. 60

chocolate fudge (Kraft Hot Fudge), 1 T. 81

chocolate fudge (Kraft Light Chocolate), 1 T. 52

chocolate fudge (Smucker's), 1 T. 60

chocolate mint (Hershey's), 1 T. 61

chocolate peanut butter (Hershey's), 1 T. 61

corn, light or dark, 1 T. 58

fudge, 1 T. 85

honey, 1 T. 64

hard sauce (Crosse and Blackwell), 1 T. 64

maple, 1 T. 50

maple flavored, buttered (Log Cabin), 1 T. 54

marshmallow, 1 T. 75

marshmallow creme (Kraft), 1 T. 45

molasses, cane, light, 1 T. 50

molasses, cane, medium, 1 T. 46

molasses, blackstrap, 1 T. 43

molasses, cane, Barbados, 1 T. 54

pecans, in syrup (Smucker's), 1 T. 90

pineapple (Kraft), 1 T. 40

sorghum, 1 T. 51

strawberry, (Kraft), 1 T. 40

table blend, cane and maple, 1 T. 50

table blend, light and dark corn, 1 T. 58

vanilla caramel, (Kraft), 1 T. 80

walnuts in syrup (Smucker's), 1 T. 80

Tacos, beef, frozen (Banquet), ½ taco as packaged 59

Tangelo juice, fresh, 6 ozs. 78

Tangerine juice,

fresh, 6 ozs. 81

canned, sweetened, 6 ozs. 93

canned, unsweetened, 6 ozs........................... 80

frozen, unsweetened, diluted, 6 ozs. 86

Tangerines,

fresh, ½ lb.. 77

fresh, 1 average, 2½″ dia. 39

Tapioca, see Puddings and Pie Fillings

Tart with fruit filling, ½ of one........................ 100

Tartar sauce, see Sauces

Tea, with 1 tsp. lemon 2

Tomato juice,

canned or bottled, 8 ozs.............................. 46

dehydrated crystals with water, 8 ozs. 49

Tomato juice cocktail, canned or bottled, 8 ozs............. 51

Tomato paste,

canned, 4 ozs. 93

canned, ¼ cup 51

Tomato puree,

canned, 4 ozs. 44

canned, ¼ cup 24

Tomatoes,

fresh, ½ lb.. 50

fresh, 1 average, 2½″ dia. 33

boiled, ½ cup....................................... 31

canned, ½ cup with liquid........................... 25

canned, stewed (Hunt's), ½ cup 32

Tongue, beef, medium fat, braised, 1 oz.................. 70

Toppings, see also Syrups

Dream Whip, 1 T. 14

marshmallow creme (Kraft), 1 T. 45

Tortilla, 1 of 3″ dia.................................... 96

Tripe, beef,

pickled, 4 ozs....................................... 70

1 medium piece, boiled 84

Trout, rainbow, canned, 1 oz.   60

Tuna, canned,

   in oil, with liquid, 1 oz.   82

   in oil, drained, 1 oz.   56

   in water pack, 1 oz. with liquid   36

Turkey,

   dark meat, roasted, 1 oz.   58

   light meat, roasted, 1 oz.   50

   giblets, simmered, 1 oz.   66

   potted, 1 oz.   71

Turnip greens,

   raw, ½ lb.   64

   boiled, small amount water, short time, drained, ½ cup   15

   boiled, large amount water, long time, drained, ½ cup   14

   canned, ½ cup with liquid.   21

   frozen, ½ cup.   22

Turnips, boiled, drained,

   ½ cup   18

   ½ cup mashed   30

TV Dinners

   chicken dishes,

      chicken, fried (Banquet), 11.2 ozs. 543

      chicken, fried (Morton), 11 ozs. 435

      chicken, fried (Swanson), 11½ ozs. 570

      chicken & noodles (Banquet), 12 ozs. 374

      chicken & noodles (Swanson), 10¼ ozs. 380

      chicken, white meat (Weight Watchers), 10 ozs. 284

      chicken livers (w/onions) (Weight Watchers), 10½ ozs. 220

      chopped chicken liver (Weight Watchers), 5 ozs. 229

   fish dishes,

      Morton dinner, 9 ozs. 375

      fish and chips (Swanson), 10¼ ozs. 450

      ocean fillet (Swanson), 11½ ozs. 440

      fish fillet, buttered (Mrs. Paul's), 1 oz. . . . .   37 haddock dinner (Banquet), 8¾ ozs. 419

ocean perch (Banquet), 8¾ ozs. 434

shrimp (Morton), 7¾ ozs. 380

flounder (Weight Watchers), 16 ozs. 268

Fille 'o' fish (Weight Watchers), 18 ozs. 266

ocean perch (Weight Watchers), 18 ozs. 307

sole (Weight Watchers), 18 ozs. 279

turbot, greenland (Weight Watchers), 18 ozs. 426

Italian style

Banquet dinner, 11 ozs. 312

Swanson dinner, 13½ ozs. 510

lasagna (Celeste), 8 ozs. 413

lasagna with veal and cheese sauce (Weight Watchers),
13 ozs. 380

manicotti (Celeste), 13 ozs. 428

ravioli, beef dinner, 4 ozs. 259

spaghetti and meatballs (Banquet), 11½ ozs. 450

spaghetti and meatballs (Morton), 11 ozs. 370

veal parmigiana

Banquet, 11 ozs. 421

Swanson, 12¼ ozs. 520

veal parmigiana and zucchini in sauce (Weight Watchers)   230

sausage, cheese and tomato pies (Weight Watchers),
2 (14 oz. pkg.) 390

Latin style,

chili con carne w/beans (Banquet cooking bag). 310

enchilada, beef and sauce (Banquet cooking bag) 259

enchilada, beef dinner (Banquet), 12 ozs. 479

International Dinner (Swanson), 15 ozs. 570

meat pies,

beef,

Banquet, 8 ozs. 409

Morton, 8 ozs. 370

Swanson, 8 ozs. 430

Swanson Deep Dish, 16 ozs. 770

chicken,

    Banquet, 8 ozs. 427

    Morton, 8 ozs. 445

    Swanson, 8 ozs. 460

    Swanson Deep Dish, 16 ozs. 750

tuna,

    Banquet, 8 ozs. 434

    Morton, 8 ozs. 385

turkey

    Banquet, 8 ozs. 415

    Morton, 8 ozs. 410

    Swanson, 8 ozs. 450

    Swanson Deep Dish, 16 ozs. 760

meat dishes,

  beef,

    Banquet, 11.2 ozs. 365

    Morton, 11 ozs. 350

    Swanson, 11½ ozs. 370

    Swanson, 3 course meal, 15 ozs. 540

  beef, chopped (Banquet), 11 ozs. 443

  beef hash, corned (Banquet), 10 ozs. 372

  beef, sliced (Morton, 3 course), 17 ozs. 563

  beef, sliced with barbecue sauce (Banquet cooking bag),

    5 ozs. 152

  beef, sliced and gravy (Banquet cooking bag), 5 ozs. 158

  beans and franks w/sauce

    Morton, 12 ozs. 554

    Banquet, 10¾ ozs. 528

    Swanson, 11¼ ozs. 550

  ham,

    Banquet, 10 ozs. 369

    Morton, 11 ozs. 385

    Swanson, 10¼ ozs. 380

  macaroni and beef, (Morton), 11 ozs. 414

macaroni and cheese,

    Banquet, 12.4 ozs.............................. 375

    Morton, 12¾ ozs. 445

meat loaf,

    Banquet, 11.2 ozs.............................. 422

    Morton, 11 ozs. 437

Salisbury steak

    Banquet, 11.2 ozs.............................. 400

    Morton, 11 ozs. 394

    Swanson, 11½ ozs............................. 500

    Swiss steak (Swanson), 10 ozs...................... 380

Oriental,

    chicken, Cantonese (Chun King), 11 ozs.............. 302

    International Entrees, Chinese (Swanson), 8½ ozs. 200

    chop suey, beef (Banquet cooking bag), 7 ozs. 121

    chop suey, beef dinner (Banquet), 12 ozs. 282

    chow mein, chicken (Banquet), 12 ozs. 282

    Polynesian Style International Entrees (Swanson), 12¼ ozs. 510

turkey,

    Banquet, 8 ozs. 415

    Morton, 8 ozs................................. 410

    Swanson, 8 ozs................................ 450

    Swanson Deep Dish, 16 ozs........................ 760

Vanilla extract, ½ tsp.   3

Veal,

    chuck, medium fat, braised, 1 oz. 67

    cutlet, 1½ oz., cooked............................. 92

    cutlet, breaded, medium, ⅓ of 1 average 100

    foreshank, medium fat, stewed, 1 oz.................. 61

    leg, roasted, 1 med. slice........................... 70

    loin, medium fat, broiled, 1 oz. 70

    plate, medium fat, stewed, 1 oz...................... 86

    rib, medium fat, roasted, 1 oz. 75

    round with rump, medium fat, broiled, 1 oz............. 61

    stew meat, 1 oz., cooked........................... 84

Vegetable juice cocktail, canned or bottled, 8 ozs.   41

Vegetables, see individual listings

Vegetables, mixed,

    frozen, ½ cup.   61

    frozen, butter sauce (Bird's Eye), ½ cup   83

Venison, lean only, raw, 1¾ oz.   69

Vinegar,

    cider, 1 T.   2

    distilled, 1 T.   2

Waffles, frozen (Aunt Jemima), ½ of a double waffle.   64

Walnuts,

    black, 8 to 10 halves   95

    English, 8 to 10 halves   98

Water chestnuts, Chinese, raw, ¼ lb.   68

Watercress,

    raw, ¼ lb..   20

    raw, 5 sprigs, ...   1

Watermelon,

    fresh, ½ lb..   20

    fresh, 1 wedge, 2½" x 2" x 1"   31

    fresh, cubes or balls, ½ cup   26

    rind, pickled, 3 pieces.   40

Welsh rarebit, 1¾ oz.   93

Wheat, see Cereals

Wheat germ, commercial

    1 T..   29

    with sugar and honey (Kretschmer), 3 T..   80

Whitefish, smoked, 2 ozs.   88

Yams, see Potatoes, sweet

Yeast,

    baker's, compressed, 1 oz.   24

    dry, active, 1 oz.   80

    Brewer's dry, debittered, 1 oz..   80

Yogurt,

    plain (Borden's), ½ cup 84

    plain, made from partially skimmed milk, ½ cup 62

    plain (Dannon), ½ cup 65

    plain, made from whole milk, ½ cup 77

    plain (Sealtest), ½ cup 72

    coffee (Dannon), ½ cup 100

    pineapple-orange (Dannon), ⅓ cup 87

    red raspberry (Dannon), ⅓ cup 87

    strawberry (Dannon), ⅓ cup 87

    vanilla (Dannon), ½ cup 100

Zucchini, see Squash, summer

Alcoholic Beverages:

Beers,

    ale, light, 8 ozs. 98

    ale, imported, 4 ozs. 76

    beer, bock, 4 ozs. 68

    beer, lager, 4 ozs. 57

    stout, 4 ozs. 73

Cider, fermented, 4 ozs. 48

Cocktails, (best to avoid altogether, but if you must imbibe,
share one with a friend!)

    Alexander, brandy, ⅓ of one 75

    Bacardi cocktail, ⅓ of one 52

    Bloody Mary, ½ 70

    Champagne cocktail, ½ 63

    daiquiri, ½ 70

    eggnog, ¼ 84

    Gimlet, ½ 68

    gin fizz, ½ 83

    grasshopper, ⅓ 78

    Manhattan, ½ 88

    Martini, ½ 68

    mint julep, ½ 100
    Old-Fashioned, ½ 73
    Orange Blossom, ½ 75
    Pink Lady, ½ 90
    Rob Roy, ½ 95
    Screwdriver, ½ 83
    Sidecar, ½ 80
    Sloe Gin Fizz, ½ 78
    Stinger, ½ 73
    Tom Collins, ½ 83
    Whiskey Sour, ½ 70

Liquors and whiskeys,
    bourbon, 1 oz. 84
    Canadian whiskey, 1 oz. 84
    gin, 1 oz. 97
    Irish whiskey, 1 oz. 84
    rum, 1 oz. 100
    rye whiskey, 1 oz. 84
    Scotch whiskey, 1 oz. 76
    Sloe gin, 1½ oz. 85
    vodka, 1 oz. 84

Liqueurs and brandies,
    anisette, 1 oz. 75
    applejack, 1 oz. 75
    Benedictine, 1 oz. 75
    brandy, California, 1 oz. 75
    brandy, cognac, 1 oz. 75
    chartreuse, 1 oz. 75
    cherry brandy, 1 oz. 90
    Cherry Heering, 1 oz. 60
    creme de cacao, 1 oz. 75
    creme de menthe, 1 oz. 90
    Curacao, 1 oz. 70
    Drambuie, 1 oz. 65

Wines,

Champagne, 3½ ozs.	90
dinner, dry, red (Chianti, Claret, Burgundy), 3½ ozs.	75
dinner, dry, white (Chablis, Moselle, Rhine), 3½ ozs.	70
dinner, white, Sauterne, 3½ ozs.	90
Dubonnet, 2 ozs.	100
Madeira, 3 ozs.	96
Malaga, 2 ozs.	100
Muscatel, 2 ozs.	92
port, 2 ozs.	92
sherry, 2 ozs.	80
vermouth, dry, 3 ozs.	96
vermouth, sweet, 2 ozs.	100

Note: Keep in mind that when you take even just one alcoholic drink, your willpower weakens so that it isn't just the added calories of a cocktail, but what it might lead to in consuming more food or additional drinks, that is the problem. It's a good idea to stop consuming alcohol while you're dieting. You'll lose weight faster and you'll be healthier for it.

10

Staying on Your Model's Diet While Eating Away from Home

One of the most difficult times to stay on a diet is when you are either traveling or eating in a restaurant. If you could just isolate yourself while you are on your diet, you would surely lose weight much faster and more successfully, but unfortunately most dieters find that they are hardly ever alone. It's hard enough when you are at home and your family puts pressure on you to eat, but when you are out, you find distractions and temptations everywhere. You have to be on guard at all times lest you succumb to the desires of your taste buds.

The best way to handle temptation is to avoid letting yourself be led in the wrong direction in the first place. If you wait until the very last moment when you have to make a decision about eating something that is not on your diet, you are much more likely to make the wrong decision. Instead, try to imagine ahead of time some of the eating situations and problems which will come up during the day. Decide beforehand what you will say and do, and you will be less likely to stray from your diet. Remember, keep yourself in control at all times!

FAST FOOD PLACES

Forget about fast food eateries while you are on your diet. Everything they serve is "off limits" for you.

Patricia R. was a "regular" at a fast food diner. Patricia always had a tendency to be "pleasingly plump," but she yearned to be the thin person she envisioned in her daydreams. One day she looked at the height/weight charts and determined that for her 5' 5" frame she should weight about 120 pounds. At that time she weighed 141 pounds.

Patricia immediately gave up her visits to the diner. It took her 2 months to lose 21 pounds. Even now she says she finds it hard to believe she is really the one she sees in a mirror or in the reflection of a store window. She still thinks of herself as a heavy person and is trying to convince herself of the truth.

At a fast food place, the food is generally fried, full of carbohydrates, and usually contains more calories than you can afford to give your body at this time. Don't tempt fate. Don't even accompany a friend into one of these places. You just can't handle it. You are going to have to pretend that these places don't exist while you're on your diet.

When you order chicken at a fast food place, it has been cooked in deep fat under pressure. In this process the fat has been forced to the very bone of the chicken so that the entire chicken is saturated with fat. A 4-ounce serving of chicken then yields over 500 calories, approximately half protein and half fat. Fish may be considered a low-calorie entree for your diet, but not when you order fried fish and chips in one of these fast food places.

Did you know that every French fried potato is worth 16 calories and every potato chip about 11 calories? One slice of pizza (an eighth of a pie) is more than 200 calories, depending on what's added to the standard cheese pizza. One quarter of a cup of potato salad is worth 92 calories.

Even the smallest hamburger has at least 250 calories, with a milkshake being about the same. About the only thing you can do if you do get stuck with having to order something in a fast food place is to order a hamburger, throw away the bun, and drink a diet soda or have an iced tea sweetened with a sugar substitute. You can survive this way, but why put yourself in the position of having to watch your friends eat all those forbidden, calorie-laden goodies? When the gang wants to go and get something to eat, try to suggest some other type of eatery, such as a coffee shop, diner or restaurant. At least there you can have some choice.

COFFEE SHOPS AND DINERS

If you are smart, you will keep a little list with you at all times that tells you what you may order if you find yourself in a coffee shop or diner. The idea is that you want to have your selection in your mind before you go in. Be knowledgeable about this so that you will be able to order fearlessly without straying too far from your diet. Menus in these places don't vary much, so your pre-selection plans should work out nicely for you.

Eliminate any kind of sandwich from your proposed list. There are just too many calories when you include bread. A grilled cheese sandwich fried in butter might have as many as 500 calories.

A 4-inch pancake has only 61 calories, and that doesn't sound too menacing to your diet, but add two more pancakes (since they usually come in a stack of three), plus three pats of butter, plus 4 tablespoons of syrup, and the total calorie count runs up to 533 calories!

You may see a "low-calorie plate" on the menu. Don't just order this blindly. It may not be as low in calories as they are leading you to believe. There are usually too many kinds of foods on such a platter, including some that are not so low-calorie. Before ordering, stop for a minute and check out exactly what you are getting and how many calories are in that food. That's why you should always carry a calorie counter with you wherever you go.

Eggs, when they're prepared properly, are always a good choice to include in your diet menus. A poached or boiled egg has only about 80 calories and a scrambled or sunny-side-up egg may have only a little over 100 calories. But beware of eggs Benedict, for there you are flirting with as much as 700 calories! Get out of the habit of having other things with your eggs, such as bacon, sausage, grits, potatoes and toast topped with butter and jam. It is possible to eat one egg, enjoy it and not go off your diet. This may take a lot of willpower because many places will not give you a lonely egg on a plate. You may have to take whatever comes with the average egg order, such as toast and potatoes. You were probably brought up by a mother who told you that you had to clean your plate or children in some foreign country would go hungry, but forget about that. Either assert yourself with the waitress and tell her you really don't want *anything else* except for one egg, or have the willpower to leave all the things you are not allowed to eat.

Most of these eating establishments will have individual boxes of dry cereal. You can eat these without milk to save calories, or if you must have your milk, ask the waitress if she has skim or low-fat milk.

Individual cans of soup may also be had in coffee shops and diners. Pick clear soups or those lowest in calorie count. Check your list of soups in the calorie counter section of this book.

A banana with a glass of skim milk makes a very tasty, nutritious meal. Sometimes other fresh fruits are available, as well as a fresh, mixed fruit salad. Some places may have side orders of cottage cheese and hard boiled eggs.

If the eating place has a salad on the menu, try to learn to eat your salads without dressing. Salt, pepper and a squeeze of lemon will substitute for a high-calorie dressing.

In choosing a beverage, it is best to stick to diet drinks or tea and coffee sweetened with artificial sweetener, because most regular soft drinks will give you about 100 calories per 8-ounce glass. Fruit juices are not always wise choices, for many 6-ounce servings have 80 calories and up. Some eating places serve a relatively low-calorie hot chocolate mix that comes in individual packages and mixes with hot water. A drink such as this may deceive your stomach and your taste buds into thinking that they are getting food as well as drink.

RESTAURANTS

To order with confidence when dining out with friends at a restaurant, you must have an idea ahead of time of just what foods you can allow yourself. Remember, you don't want your friends to make suggestions; you have to be in charge of your selection. You have to be very definite and assertive when you announce, "I know what *I* want." If suggestions are made, you can get out of it by saying, "I had that for lunch yesterday," or, "Yes, that sounds good, but I don't feel like it right now." Never admit that your diet won't allow it. You are acting by your own choice.

As you look over the list of entrees at a fine restaurant, everything sounds delicious, but you must not be influenced by those sweet-talking adjectives on the menu. You have to be discriminating and knowledgeable about what you may order.

The most important thing to remember as you scan the menu is to forget about ordering from the dinner side. So many things automatically come with a dinner that you may be tempted to eat simply because you are paying for them in the overall price of the dinner. Always order á la carte. Although it may sometimes cost you more money to do this, it is worth it for your diet's sake. Nowadays, with so many people on diets, you won't suffer any embarrassment with the waiter if you order lightly from the á la carte side of the menu instead of having a complete dinner.

Stay away from all choices that are fried, breaded or heavily laced with rich sauces. In many fine restaurants the sauce is added just before it is served, so it is easy to decline. A large shrimp cocktail can suffice as a complete meal. If a restaurant only has the small shrimp cocktail on the menu that they usually serve before the actual meal, ask the waitress if it is possible to have an order of six or more large shrimp on a bed of lettuce.

Many restaurants have a salad bar where you can prepare your own plate. This can easily be an entire meal and low in calories if you avoid the rich dressings and choose things like hard boiled eggs, bean sprouts, cottage cheese, cole slaw, tomatoes, mixed greens, fruit salad and jello.

If your job or business requires that you take people out to restaurants for lunch or dinner often, it certainly will be of help to you to memorize or make a small list that you can keep with you to help you order the things that will keep you slim.

DINING AS A GUEST

If you are eating out at a good restaurant because you are being entertained, you will have to break your 600 calorie diet, but at least, if you follow my suggestions, you won't be going overboard with too many excess calories. When ordering your entree, choose fish that has been broiled, a small filet mignon, or chicken. Always remove the skin from the chicken and trim off any visible fat on any meat entree that you may order.

Learn to like eating a baked potato without the trimmings. A small baked potato is only about 90 calories, but when you add a couple of pats of butter, a teaspoon of bacon bits, a spoonful of grated cheese and a blob of sour cream on top, it adds up to almost 300 calories!

For a salad, ask the waiter if you can have three or four slices of tomato on some lettuce instead of the regular salad with house dressing. Any green vegetable will fit into your diet plan if you do not add butter. For dessert most restaurants have fresh fruit, jello without whipped cream, and sherbet. If you follow this plan when ordering, you won't go away from the table hungry and you won't stray too far from your diet.

ALCOHOLIC DRINKS

Alcohol should never be a part of any reducing diet because it furnishes too many empty calories and also increases your appetite. If you find yourself in a situation where you really want to drink something, try white wine instead of liquor. This will not only cut down on your liquor intake, but will also lessen your calorie count. It is no wonder that people who drink a lot get fat, for if the alcohol is not burned up immediately, it is deposited directly into the body as fat. The body does not treat alcohol as a carbohydrate in its metabolic process.

EATING WHILE ON VACATION

It is possible to continue losing weight while on a vacation, but it is rather unlikely, for every day you are being thrown into new, unknown situations with temptation beckoning everywhere you turn. The best you can do, first of all, is to eliminate the thought of going on an ocean cruise or visiting any place that features a fine cuisine as their main attraction. No need to put stumbling blocks in your own path. Almost everyone comes back from a trip of this sort over-weight by 5 or even 10 pounds. Eating becomes a pastime, part of the recreational calendar, instead of being kept in its proper perspective of furnishing nourishment for your body. You eat because it is there and is prepared so tastily and displayed so attractively.

Because it is almost impossible to lose weight while on a vacation, try to do the next best thing—maintain the weight you are at right now. This will be difficult enough for you, but just keep in mind that you didn't go on vacation to eat; you went to see and experience new things. Eating is for survival, not pleasure. Just follow the same plan you use for eating out at home and you'll get through your vacation very nicely without any added pounds. Keep a calorie counter with you at all times. If you can, try to plan what you are going to eat ahead of time and actually write out menus for yourself with the approximate calorie counts.

OTHER PLACES TO EAT OUT

Besides restaurants, diners and coffee shops, there are other places where we are faced with the situation of eating away from home. It has become a habit to eat something while sitting in a movie theater. Convince yourself that the candy bars are all undersized and overpriced (that's not hard to do!) and if you must—I mean really *must*—have something to nibble on, buy the smallest size order of popcorn without the butter. Popcorn without butter is only 54 calories per cup.

Try to stay away from fairs and carnivals. There is too much food being offered everywhere you look. If you have to go, be sure to eat beforehand and keep telling yourself how full you are every time the suggestion to eat comes your way.

You won't want to stay away from your favorite sporting event, but you also don't want to eat there. Remind yourself that you don't eat between meals, you never eat hot dogs with a bun—and most important—you didn't come to eat, you came to watch, cheer on your team and have a good time.

When special occasions come up where refreshments are served at the PTA or at church, remember what the occasion or celebration is for and concentrate on that. Remind yourself that you didn't come to see how much food you could consume. Allow yourself one cup of punch and make it last for the entire time you are there. This will give you something to hold in your hand while you are visiting and chatting with other people.

When you are away from home and have to eat, remember the following:

- *You* are in control of your life at all times.
- Plan what you are going to eat in advance.
- Keep a food diary and count your calories.
- Try to eat new foods and food combinations if the calorie count is within your limit.
- Concentrate on and enjoy the things you are doing.

11

Staying on Your Model's Diet
When You Are a Guest

During the first few weeks of your diet, you may not be too sure of your willpower. If that is the case, you will want to avoid all social contacts that include eating. You will have to be the judge.

THE COCKTAIL PARTY

It is really best not to eat at all at a cocktail party. If you are on a diet to maintain your weight and not to lose weight, you might be able to carry it off, but if you are trying desperately to lose weight, then put food out of your mind. Do this before you leave home. Just remind yourself that you are going to the cocktail party to see old friends and make new ones and to have a good time. You are not going for the purpose of eating anything, because a cocktail party takes place between meals and *you* don't eat between meals. You are also not going to the cocktail party to drink and get high. You don't need to get high to have a good time. Sure, you can drink something, but not alcohol. Liquor has too many calories. A martini has 135 calories, a Tom Collins has 165 calories and a Scotch-and-soda made with 1 ounce of Scotch has 76 calories.

Have a club soda, mineral water or a low-calorie beverage. It is best to avoid alcohol when you're dieting because otherwise it increases your appetite and takes away your inhibitions, including watching your consumption of calories. You don't need the peanuts, chips, pretzels, caviar and high-calorie hors d'oeuvres. You have to understand that, on a calorie count of 600 calories per day, you cannot consume alcoholic beverages that steal 80 to 100 calories per drink from your nutrition. Even if you limit yourself to one drink per day, you are still losing those calories which would have provided your body with the nutrients it must have to function properly. You are already trying to make your body perform on less calories than it needs so that it will be burning off the fat that you've acquired. It would be unhealthy to deprive it even more. Find a substitute for alcohol, such as a glass of plain soda water with a twist of lemon. Perrier and other brands of mineral water are extremely popular with the "in" crowd. If you must drink alcohol, always leave some liquid in the bottom of your glass so that you are free to say that you are not ready for another drink yet.

THE BUFFET DINNER

If you learn to control what you put into your body, eating sensibly at all times, you can have your cake and eat it too. Most parties these days are served buffet style, so you can take as much or as little food as you please. Unless you really talk about your dieting problems a lot, other people will not even notice what you are putting on your plate or what you are rejecting. Because we are all pretty much self-centered, you are more aware than others of what you are actually eating. Other people are just as self-centered as you are, and they will be more interested in what they are putting on their plates than in what you are putting on yours. After they fill their plates as full as they can get without spilling anything, they are not going to be concerned with how much you have on yours or what you are eating. If you don't believe me, just watch the people around you after they get their plates full. They will be so involved in digging into what they have selected, eating heartily and perhaps going back for seconds, that you might as well be the invisible man! Nibble on your diet platter and enjoy.

In choosing what you will eat there are two things you must be knowledgeable about:

- Approximately how many calories are in the food you want to eat.

- What foods your body requires to stay in good physical condition.

If you only observe one of these principles, you are in trouble. If you only know about nutrition and what your body demands, but you know nothing about the calorie count of various foods, your diet will fail because many things which are healthy for you are also quite fattening. If you know nothing about nutrition and only choose low-calorie foods to eat because you know the calorie count, you may be starving your body of nutrients and damaging your physical condition. Both factors have to work hand in hand.

As you go through the buffet line, put a lot of lettuce on your plate. It makes your plate look full and you can eat as much of it as you like; or, on the other hand, if you don't want to eat it all, it is perfectly acceptable to leave it on your plate as many people do, using it as something to lay other food on rather than eating it. Choose foods that make your plate look fuller than it really is. When you put food on your plate, spread it around so that it looks like more. Take some of all of the salad fixings you are offered, such as carrot curls, cucumber slices, cottage cheese, sliced tomatoes, green pepper sticks and cole slaw. You can have small servings of the sliced ham, chicken or other meat. Avoid hot rolls and crackers. If there is fresh fruit, fruit salad or jello on the buffet table, you may have some, but if not, pass on the desserts.

Take small bites and chew your food well. This tip will make the small amount of food on your plate seem like as much as what those around you are having. By chewing your food well before swallowing it, you are not only making it last longer, but you are also helping the digestive processes by starting the enzymes flowing. After you are on your diet for a while, you will not desire the large amounts of food you craved before.

Do you remember what it was like when you used to eat until you were so full that you couldn't take another bite? It wasn't a pleasure any more, was it? You felt groggy, lethargic and uncomfortable. You don't need that. You want to retain your pep and vitality, so try to take a new point of view in regard to your dieting.

Remember, weight control is 90 percent attitude. If you really want to be thin, you should try being a "gourmet dieter," eating small amounts of food but savoring each mouthful. You may even be surprised yourself when you see how easy this is once it becomes a habit with you.

THE SIT-DOWN DINNER

If you feel that you can handle being invited out to a sit-down dinner at someone's house, try to find out ahead of time what will be served. If what your hostess plans to serve is extremely fattening, it may be possible for her to provide a substitution for you without too much extra trouble. If you are an absolute coward and hesitate discussing an alternative food choice, then you may be better off visiting after everyone is done eating. Explain to her that you simply cannot cope with a dinner invitation right now, that you really want to come and have a pleasant visit with everyone and would she mind if you came over after dinner is finished. This may bring a response like, "This one time won't make any difference to your diet. You mustn't diet all the time. You'll lose your strength and get sick!" Friends don't understand you if they say things like that. Any time you eat something that you shouldn't makes a difference to your diet and your body suffers for it. The food you put into your mouth and the pleasure you get from it cannot be worth what you have to do to get rid of those extra consumed calories. Of course you have to realize that your hostess is probably not as well educated as you are when it comes to knowing about the calorie counts of foods and what you have had to deprive yourself of to lose weight. You mustn't blame her. She means well. She is doing her job as a gracious hostess in trying to provide all the things she believes will satisfy and give pleasure to her guests.

Only you can decide what you should tell your hostess once she reveals what she is planning to serve. Of course, you can't say to a good friend, "I'm not going to come. You're not serving anything I like to eat." (Or rather, "You're not serving anything I can eat on my diet.") You'd sound like a spoiled brat. Sometimes it's better not to draw attention to the fact that you're on a diet. Well-meaning friends usually wind up making remarks that hinder your dieting rather than help it.

Yes, eating is definitely a pleasure, but remember that food should be secondary. The main reason friends get together is because they like each other's company. You must never go to any dinner or party grimly determined to avoid almost everything in sight. This takes away from your fun and accentuates the negative thoughts you may be having. After the party is over, you may feel so deprived that you will stuff yourself with whatever you can find in your refrigerator upon returning home. The frustrated dieter will eat almost anything.

Try, if you can, to concentrate on enjoying the people you came to see. Spark a new interest with each individual you speak to. Then you can forget about the importance of eating. You might even enjoy eating some foods that you don't particularly like—if they fit in with your diet plan. You may not be able to eat everything the hostess serves, but you don't have to refuse an invitation entirely. You can cope. Keep telling yourself that and you'll believe it.

At many dinner parties, your appetite can get out of control if dinner is delayed beyond the expected hour. If you have reason to believe that this may happen, try to cut your appetite before you leave home by having a glass of milk, a cup of clear soup or a hard cooked egg. This will save you from appeasing a stomach crying out to be fed if dinner is late.

Some people think that, by eating a diet of only protein food, they will not only avoid gaining weight, but will also lose some. Important as protein is, if it is to be burned up properly by the body and have its maximum efficiency, there must also be carbohydrate present. So you see, foods which contain carbohydrates are not always the villains they appear to be.

Try not to salt food which is served to you. Every cook always seasons the food while it is being prepared. Let that be your guide. You don't need more. Low salt intake is very important to losing weight. Too much salt makes the body retain water.

If your hostess wants to give you more food than you are ready to accept, don't be too embarrassed to say "no." It is no longer considered ill-mannered to turn down food or drink, for most modern hostesses understand that many people are on reducing diets and a hostess will want to cooperate in making her guests feel as comfortable as possible. A good hostess will always include some low-calorie food among her refreshments so that all of her guests will be able to enjoy what she has prepared.

EATING WHEN YOU ARE A HOUSEGUEST

When you are invited to be someone's houseguest, you will be offered hospitality at its best. Every hostess wants to make a really fine impression on her guests, whether she can afford to entertain two or 22. If you know your hostess well enough, it may be a good idea to give her a list ahead of time of common foods you can eat and still stay on your diet. Make it a point to inform her that you are not a heavy eater and she doesn't have to go to a lot of trouble just for you. Tell her that your tastes are simple; you don't go in for rich and fancy dishes. Give her an idea of what you normally eat for a meal. It may be hard for her to accept what you are telling her. It's a hostess's prime duty to feed her guests well, and what you are describing sounds so skimpy to her, it may make her feel cheap to cooperate with you. Prepare yourself to describe the tremendous struggle you are putting up and how important it is that you stay on your diet. Say to her, "I know it's hard for you to accept what I am telling you, but it's hard enough for me to stay on my diet even when I have the cooperation of others. If you think well of me at all, you'll cooperate and not feed me things I shouldn't have."

It is normal for your appetite to be whetted by walking into a beautiful dining room where the table is set with lovely linen, expensive crystal, elegant dinnerware and fine silver. Any kind of food appears more attractive in a setting like this. Sometimes atmosphere can be more important than the food itself. When the mood is right, people will enjoy themselves, no matter what kind of food is put before them. You must always be especially on guard in circumstances such as these. But, on the other hand, you will also be able to enjoy staying on your diet and being satisfied with less, low-calorie foods.

When you are a houseguest, offer to go along when the hostess shops for food and select things which are good for your diet. When you do this, always offer to pay for your selections. She will probably not accept, but it would be polite to make the offer, since you may be selecting things that she had no intention of buying.

Make sure that your hostess has all the makings of the snacks you need. Help her to prepare them so that they will be in the refrigerator, and ready to eat at a moment's notice. Things like celery, green pepper strips, carrot sticks and radishes can be prepared ahead of time and nibbled on for days. They can also be a part of any meal.

CARD PARTIES

Drink diet soda, chew gum, but don't eat any of those snacks that may find their way beside your elbow. If a luncheon is served, eat only the things that you know you are allowed to have. Find out ahead of time what will be served. It might not be a bad idea to bring your own lunch, put it in the kitchen when you arrive and have it served on the same plates as everyone else. It will hardly be noticed.

If all of your friends are stuffing themselves with those gigantic submarine sandwiches and beer, you'll have to content yourself with the contents of the sandwich and throw away the loaf-size bread it comes with. Drink anything that is low-calorie. Lemonade with a non-nutritive sweetener such as Sweet and Low quenches your thirst just as well as beer and has hardly any calories at all.

Just remember, the purpose of getting together is not to eat food, but to play a game. Concentrate on playing a better game and you'll come out a winner—if not with your game, then at least with your diet!

GETTING THROUGH THE HOLIDAYS

Celebrating most holidays means overeating. Fourth of July and Labor Day picnics, dinners for Easter, Passover, Christmas and Thanksgiving, can all mean the downfall to your diet if you don't prepare yourself to cope with them. Your willpower must be made of steel in order to get you through days like these. Special food and an abundance of it highlights every holiday, especially Thanksgiving. How do you survive?

Usually, you'll know ahead of time what you will be presented with at the dinner table for each special holiday. Food is traditional and there are usually no new recipes or menus. Knowing this before you go to eat enables you to decide just what you will choose for your plate and how much of it. To keep your suffering to a minimum, place a teaspoonful of every food on your plate. That way, you can taste all the good things you normally eat and you won't eat too much of anything. You'll be surprised how much food that can be. It will cover your plate. You don't need more food than that. (Remember now, I said a teaspoon, not a gravy ladle.)

GO OUT, EAT AND ENJOY LIFE

It's true that eating is a large part of the fun of any party. Food has become the center of our lives. All hostesses like to serve their guests the very best they can afford in plentiful amounts. Food that is served to guests is usually richer than what you normally eat every day. Who wants to go to a party to eat everyday food?

You, of course, are very conscious of the fact that you are dieting, but you are not alone in giving food the attention it gets. It's quite natural to be thinking about food—what it looks like, how it smells, how it feels in your mouth, how it tastes and how it makes you feel after you've eaten it.

Eating should be a delightful experience even when you are counting calories, but prime importance should be given to the nourishment of your body. When you choose what you will eat, try to maintain the balance of the joy you get from eating with the nutrition you are providing your body. Control your calories. Don't let them control you! You must not associate good eating with overeating.

It really isn't necessary to give up having a good time with your friends just because you are on a reducing diet. Be kind to yourself! Go to the cocktail parties, go to those suppers, go to your card parties, go on a weekend visit with your friends. Go, but be prepared. Know ahead of time just what you will eat and what you will not eat. This goes for drinking, too. With the right attitude, you'll have as much fun as you ever did before.

12

How to Overcome Fatigue During Your Diet

It's extremely difficult to look beautiful when you feel tired. Dark shadows under the eyes mar a usually clear complexion and lines show up where there were none before. Besides the visual aspects of fatigue, it makes you lose interest, not only in yourself, but also in the wonderful world around you. Feeling half alive takes all the fun out of life, draining you of your energies and talents.

WHY ARE YOU SO TIRED?

The most logical explanation of fatigue is that it is the result of doing hard physical work, but this is not why most of us feel tired all the time. Fatigue is often a warning signal or a symptom telling you that you are actually ill. This is why I always advise anyone planning to go on a reducing diet to consult a doctor first. Make sure you are in reasonably good health and then proceed.

Tiredness can often be caused by *anemia*. There are several kinds of anemia, the most common among women being a deficiency in iron which can usually be corrected by diet and by taking an iron supplement until the condition clears up. Because even mild anemia can be the prelude to a serious disease, it should be checked by your doctor, without trying to treat it yourself.

One of the earliest symptoms of *heart trouble* is unexplained weakness or fatigue. It can come as a warning either weeks or months in advance of an attack.

Anything interfering with the lungs' ability to deliver enough oxygen to the blood, or the blood's circulation to the tissues can cause fatigue. One of the earliest signs of *lung disease* is hyperventilation with its breathlessness and accompanying tiredness.

Hyperventilation is a disorder that affects approximately one fifth of all adults, most of them women. It develops over a period of several years, with the victim subconsciously overbreathing and thereby releasing too much carbon dioxide from the body. Besides fatigue, it can also produce dizziness, nausea, palpitations and chest pain.

About 13 percent of the adult population is affected by *thyroiditus*, a chronic inflammation of the thyroid gland located in the neck. One fourth of these cases progress on to nearly complete thyroid destruction and a condition called *hypothyroidism*. Since the thyroid hormone plays such an important role in so many body regulating processes, the lack of it produces many symptoms, one of which is fatigue. Some of the others are lethargy, dry skin, puffiness of the face, chronic irritability, constipation and irregular menstrual periods.

Hypoglycemia is a disorder caused by low blood sugar and not only produces tiredness in its victims, but also shakiness, heart palpitations and impaired ability to concentrate. It can usually be corrected with a high protein, low carbohydrate diet.

Hypercalcemia is a condition caused by an elevated blood calcium level and can go on to produce serious complications, such as kidney stones, peptic ulcers, hypertension, leg muscle weakness and mental confusion. It can also be caused by taking too much vitamin A or D. Other symptoms, besides fatigue, are excessive thirst, frequency of urination, nausea, constipation and a general run-down feeling.

Exclusively affecting women, *metabolic edema* is caused by a hormonal imbalance and causes wide swings in body weight, swollen ankles and abdominal bloating. Little is known about this condition, but it is believed to be related to diabetes. It can be brought on by emotional stress, menstrual periods, or standing on the feet for too long. It's probably the most logical cause of unexplained swelling in women. Drugs which help the body to rid itself of excess salt and water help minimize the symptoms.

Mononucleosis is a virus infection which causes a swelling of the lymph glands and changes in the white blood cells. Fatigue is a common complaint and fever, headache and sore throat accompany it. Recovery usually takes from three to six weeks.

Not all *liver disease* causes yellow discoloration of the skin and eyeballs. Mild cases of liver disease may exhibit symptoms of fatigue, poor appetite and discomfort under the right rib cage.

Folic acid, like iron, must be in the diet because it is an essential element and cannot be manufactured by the body. A deficiency of this substance is usually found in alcoholics and patients with chronic diarrhea. A newly found cause seems to be birth control pills. More than a third of women taking birth control pills have been found to have low folic acid levels in their blood. Besides fatigue, the symptoms include numbness of the hands and feet and a mild burning sensation of the tongue.

It is generally believed that one out of three persons has some degree of *depression*. Persons with mild depression feel tired all the time and are discouraged to try to do better with their lives. They seem to get no pleasure out of life, not even leisure activities. Their attitude is, "What's the use? I'm never going to amount to anything. Things are never going to get better." It is possible for persons with mild depression to cure themselves by getting hope back into their lives. Instead of having negative thoughts, try looking at every situation in the most positive way you can imagine. Say to yourself when you get up in the morning, "This is going to be a good, meaningful day for me. I'm so lucky to be alive!" Think the same thoughts throughout your day and if things don't go exactly as you planned them, convince yourself that things will be better the next time. Stop yourself every time you find your mind drifting into negative thoughts. To get your mind off your emotions, try getting interested in some sport that you used to like, one in which you can actually participate. Regular exercise can help you get rid of depression and its accompanying tired feeling. Work this into your schedule at once even if you don't feel motivated in the beginning.

Poor posture can cause not only tiredness, but back pain and foot ailments as well. Try to imagine yourself as a puppet with a string holding you erect from the center of your head. Your shoulders should be relaxed, chest high and buttocks tucked under. Use your muscles to hold in your abdomen. Take pride in your posture and try to develop graceful movement as you walk. Be aware of good posture habits when you are sitting as well as standing and walking. Sit tall and don't slouch. Crossing the legs may make them look better, but if done for long periods this can cut off circulation. Try placing the feet together on the floor with one foot just ahead of the other.

Here are some *hints for a healthy back*. Point your toes straight ahead when you walk, putting most of the weight on your heels. If you have to lift anything heavy, bend your knees, squat and lift with your thigh muscles. Never bend over with your knees straight and lift with the upper torso. Move slowly and avoid sudden movements. Try to avoid lifting loads in front of you above the waistline. Avoid bending over to lift heavy objects from car trunks, as this places a strain on the lower back muscles. Sleep on a firm mattress. Don't sleep on your stomach, but instead lie on your side, keeping hips and knees bent. A ¾" plywood bedboard under the mattress can be used to give support to the back. When driving your car, sit close to the wheel with your knees bent. On long trips, stop every one or two hours and walk to relieve tension and relax muscles.

Some fatigue may be caused by *insomnia*, the inability to sleep. At least 50 percent of the people in the United States complain that they have trouble, part of the time or all of the time, going to sleep at night. Because of this affliction, many have turned to sleeping pills and have become addicted to them. You don't have to do this. First of all, stop worrying about not being able to sleep. Learn how to relax instead. Bedtime is not the appropriate time to think about all the problems you had during the day, replaying them over and over in your mind, trying to work out solutions. Don't take tomorrow to bed with you tonight, either. Worrying about problems that may come up during the next day doesn't solve them, it just makes you tense and unable to sleep. If you must plan tomorrow's day, try to do it at least two hours before your bedtime.

To prepare yourself for a good night's sleep, dress so that you are comfortable. Don't wear anything that fits too tightly. Clothes should keep you warm when it is cold and cool when it is warm. If you are more comfortable sleeping without anything on, then do so.

Consider your sleeping conditions. Your bedroom should be dark and free from outside sounds that might distract you. It should not be too hot or too cold. If you think your mattress is keeping you awake, maybe it's time you bought a new one. Most people claim that they get better rest on a firm mattress.

Allow enough time for sleeping. Don't stay out all night drinking and living it up and then expect to fall into bed and sleep soundly until your alarm goes off in the morning. Alcohol in small amounts can relax you and help you sleep, but too much may disturb your normal sleep pattern, causing you to go to sleep for two or three hours and then wake up, unable to go back to sleep again.

Don't eat just before going to bed unless it's a glass of warm milk or a bowl of hot soup. A warm bath is relaxing and may help induce sleep.

Once you are in bed, try to let go of all thoughts of the day's activities or what you are going to do tomorrow. Put your brain in neutral.

Lie on your back in your bed. Make believe your body is very heavy and the bed is very soft and you are sinking into it. Take a few deep breaths, then breathe gently. Tense your arms and stretch them out as long as you can, spreading your fingers and making them as rigid as you can. Now clench your fingers into a tight fist. Relax your fingers and arms, letting them come to rest at your sides. Think of them as very loose and floppy like a rag doll. Bring your knees up to your chest, one at a time, tensing them as you do and then dropping them down, relaxed, as you did with your arms. Rotate each foot in one direction and then the other. Relax. Roll your head from side to side several times and then pretend that it is very heavy and sinking deep into your pillow. Close your eyes tightly. Open them. Relax. Do this several times. Think of calm things, such as black velvet darkness, floating along on the clouds, lying on the beach listening to the tide go in and out, lying in the grass watching the leaves on the tree above you sway in the wind. Whenever personal matters start to creep into this relaxing mood, immediately make an effort to put them out of your mind, substituting a new "calm" picture to take its place. Whatever you do, don't worry about falling asleep, as this in itself may keep you awake. Realize that just lying quietly, relaxing and trying to fall asleep is almost as beneficial as sleep itself.

Because a lack of exercise can make you feel fatigued, exercising moderately can refresh you and relieve your tiredness. Here are some exercises that are particularly effective for this:

Lie on back, knees bent, arms at sides of body. Raise buttocks off the ground. Lower slowly. Relax. Do 5 times.

Get down on hands and knees. Take a deep breath and relax. Let head hang down, pull stomach in and curve back upward. Now arch back and raise head up. Relax. Repeat 5 times.

Sit down with knees drawn up toward chest. Clasp hands behind head. Twist right elbow to the right side of right knee, stretching as much as you can. Back to first position and relax. Now twist left elbow to the left of left knee. Stretch as much as you can. Return to first position and relax. Do 5 times on each side.

Stand with feet apart, hands clasped behind buttocks. Bend over forward from the waist and pull arms away from buttocks as far as you can. Repeat 5 times.

Stand with feet apart. Bend forward from the waist and touch fingers to ground. Walk forward with hands, keeping feet stationary. Now walk back to the starting position. Do 5 times.

Sit Indian style, clasp ankles from underneath. Bend head forward as far as you can go, trying to touch ground.

Sit with hands behind you, supporting you as you lean slightly back. Bend one knee quickly and then straighten. Do the same with the other leg. Movements should be continuous and fast.

13

Special Exercises
for Special Beautifying Effects

Nobody goes on a reducing diet to lose weight just to be thin. Being thin doesn't automatically make you beautiful. The curves must be in the right places and you must work at it if you hope to be not only slender, but healthy and beautiful. This is why it is essential to have an exercise program along with any weight loss plan, especially one made just for your figure and for no one else. Since no two people have identical figure problems, you cannot follow another person's plan. You will have to devise your own.

Think back to the day when I told you to evaluate your body by looking into the mirror, making a note of both the good and the bad features. I hope you made a list. We will use exercise to accentuate the positive traits of your body and to eliminate or diminish the negative ones. Once you determine these distinctions yourself, you can choose the exercises from this chapter to make up your own personal routine.

NO NEED FOR STRENUOUS EXERCISE

Many people erroneously think of exercise as strenuous and hard work. It needn't be. In fact, I don't believe in that at all. You should not push your body so hard with exercise that it makes you miserable. Successful exercise will make you feel more alive and actually seem to charge you with more energy than you had before you started. You must be happy when you exercise. No program of self-improvement is going to be successful if you feel forced to do something. Look forward to your exercise time as you would look forward to a special occasion or going to a dance. A special occasion it truly is, for every day you will be moving toward your goal of having a lovelier, healthier body. Not only should you try to put yourself into a happy frame of mind, but direct your thoughts to the fact that you are getting better and better every day in every way.

Your exercise clothing should not restrict you from moving freely, as this will annoy you and distract you from carrying out your exercises efficiently with a happy attitude. Dress comfortably, without anything that is tight, such as shorts or slacks with tight waistbands. A leotard is best, as you can observe your body as you exercise and, when your results start showing, you will be aware of them more quickly than if you had worn something more concealing. If you can't find a leotard at your local department store, look in the yellow pages of your telephone book under dancing supplies. If the town where you live is too small to have such a place, try a dance studio. They stock leotards and other dance items for their students.

CHOOSING A PLACE TO EXERCISE

Robert Burns once noted in one of his poems how much good it would do us all if we could only see ourselves as others see us. That's why it's a good idea to have plenty of mirrors in your home so that you can be aware of what you look like at all times. A full-length 3-way mirror is great for studying your figure as you progress with your diet and exercise program. Find a spot where you will have room to do all of your exercises without bumping into furniture. If you have to move a chair or a table, do it before you start and let nothing interrupt you from your routine. Try to exercise in the same place every day. I like to exercise in my living room because it not only is the largest spot for working out, but I can also observe myself in the mirrors covering one wall as I go through my daily schedule of exercise. I also have a large mirror outdoors in my patio area so that when weather permits and I feel so inclined, I can exercise outdoors as well. You might also find this pleasant. You can bolt a large mirror about 4 feet by 5 feet to a wall on the side or back of your house for this purpose and it will also make your yard more attractive when you entertain outdoors. The weather doesn't seem to injure a good plate glass mirror installed this way. Mine has lasted for many years without any weather spots forming. It's better to exercise with a mirror in front of you because you can study your body as you exercise and say to yourself, "Yes! I can see that I am getting better, I *do* look better than I did yesterday. I know I have a long way to go yet, but I know what I am doing is making me a more beautiful, vibrant person." You must always concentrate on positive thoughts when you exercise. The mind is a powerful thing when it is controlled and you *can* control it to help you form your body in a more attractive package. Never think any negative or critical thoughts when you exercise your body or your exercises will not have as much of a desirable effect. Mind and body must be attuned to each other and cooperate for the end purpose of making you more perfect!

Now let's get you started with one of the simplest and easiest of exercises. Just stand with your feet apart, hands clasped behind your buttocks. Bend over forward from your waist and pull your arms away from your buttocks as far as you can. Repeat this movement five times. (See Figure 1.)

There is one set of exercises that I recommend for *everyone*. These are the exercises that firm and flatten the stomach. No matter what your other figure faults may be, if you have put on excess weight you have abused this area of your body. It's a good idea, then, for you to start each of your exercise periods with stomach exercises. Your stomach is the first place you put on weight, and it should be the first place you lose weight. Makes sense, doesn't it?

When you overeat, you stretch your insides so full of food that your internal organs stretch out of shape. A bloated, misshapen stomach is the badge of an overindulgent person. Get rid of that before anything else. Why broadcast how little self-control you have and how weak-willed you are? Getting rid of or at least minimizing the size of your stomach will make you appear thinner quicker, so that's why you should place stomach exercises at the top of your list, whoever you may be. You'll want to do these every day for the rest of your life, even after all of your excess weight is gone. Start out by doing each one 5 times. When you can do 5 easily, start doing 10

Figure 1

each day. You may want to do as many as 15, but there is no need to overdo. Exercise is most helpful when done regularly and it is *what* you do that produces results, not how many times you do it or how tired you get from doing it. Always remember that exercise should not be tiring, so don't try to compete with a friend on how many times you can do a certain exercise and don't try to set any records.

EXERCISES FOR THE STOMACH

Lie down on your back, legs together, arms at sides of body. Slowly raise your legs until they are perpendicular (at a right angle) to your body. Now lower them to the floor slowly. If, due to lack of previous exercise, you cannot raise your legs to begin with, then exert yourself and swing your legs up into position quickly. You should be able to do that. Now attempt to lower them slowly. Don't let them drop suddenly to the floor near the end, but hold a steady pace and rhythm throughout the exercise. You'll be able to feel your stomach muscles tighten as you do this. (See Figures 2a, 2b, and 2c.)

Figure 2a

Figure 2b

Figure 2c

Lie flat on your back, arms overhead, legs together. Sit up and touch your toes with your fingertips. Do not arch the back, as that weakens and stretches the abdominal muscles. The back must stay flat on the floor, rolling it up smoothly with no sudden thrust to cause strain. After you master the situp with your arms overhead, try doing it with your hands at your sides. Always keep the feet touching the floor.

Lie flat on back. Use a chair to prop your feet. Raise up your body and touch your toes with your fingertips. Because the legs are propped up, abdominal muscles have to work against gravity for a more strenuous workout than in the traditional toe-touch exercise. Don't bend knees.

Lie on stomach, arms stretched out from the shoulders. Keep legs straight. Raise both shoulders and legs as high as possible from the floor.

Stand, keep arms at sides of body. As you draw in a breath, tighten your abdominal muscles, pulling your stomach in as far as possible. Now let out the air and let your stomach completely relax.

My friend Stephanie wanted to take off 10 pounds fast so that she could wear her bikini bathing suit without bulging out of it at the stomach line. She exercised every day using the stomach muscle building exercises and faithfully followed the Amazing 600 Calorie Model's Diet for two and a half weeks. The results?—a flat tummy and whistles when she walked down the beach!

FOR THE WAISTLINE

Stand with legs apart. Put left hand on left hip. Take right hand and stretch overhead, reaching to the left side of your body as far as you can. Bounce to the count of 1-2-3. Now do it on the opposite side.

Stand erect, arms at sides and legs apart. Reach over with your right hand and touch your left knee. Go back to original position. Now do the other side. Do this exercise as quickly as you can.

Stand erect, arms at sides, legs together. Swing arms overhead and then touch toes without bending the knees.

Stand erect with arms stretched out at sides. Twist body from the waist to the right and back to first position. Now twist to the left.

Lie face down, bend legs and grab ankles. Keep legs apart. Pull up as far from the floor as you can, raising head at the same time. Rock your body. Relax and do it over 4 more times.

Sit down with knees drawn up toward chest. Clasp hands behind head. Twist your right elbow to the right side of your right knee, stretching as much as you can. Back to first position and relax. Now twist your left elbow to the left of your left knee. Stretch as much as you can. Return to first position and relax. Do 5 times on each side. (See Figure 3.)

Figure 3

FOR THE HIPS

Lie flat on floor, face down, arms bent, elbows at waist, hands flat at shoulders. Raise right leg up, without bending it, as far back as possible. Stretch your muscles. Bring leg back to floor. Repeat with left leg.

Lie on back, knees bent, arms at sides of body. Raise buttocks off the ground. Lower slowly. Relax. Do 5 times. (See Figure 4.)

Lie on right side, right elbow bent under head, left hand resting on floor for support. With both legs slightly raised off the floor, pretend you are riding a bicycle and pedal vigorously for 5

Figure 4

---

counts. Be sure to keep the body in line. Don't bend in the middle. Roll to opposite side and repeat exercise.

Stand erect, hands on hips, and bend right leg. Straighten leg. Now place all of your weight on right leg and lift left leg to the front of your body as high as it will go. Lower. Now lift left leg to the left as high as it will go. Lower. Next, lift left leg to the rear as high as it will go, always keeping leg straight. Lower. Repeat with other leg, putting weight now on the left side. This exercise will also benefit your thighs.

Stand erect. Place the back of a straight chair toward you and rest your right leg on its back. Clasp your hands behind your head and bend forward as far as you can, trying to touch your knee with your elbow. Repeat with other leg.

Lie on back, arms out shoulder height, knees close together to chest. Roll knees to right side, then back to chest, then to left side. Try to keep shoulders flat on floor, just moving hips.

FOR THE THIGHS

Lie on right side, right arm folded under head, legs straight and together, left arm straight out. Keep left leg straight and lift it up as high as it will go. Lower. Repeat with other leg.

Stand with feet apart. Bend forward from the waist and touch fingers to ground. Walk forward with your hands, keeping your feet stationary. Now walk back to the starting position. Do 5 times. (See Figure 5.)

Figure 5

Sit on ground, hands behind you, supporting you as you lean slightly back. Bend one knee quickly and then straighten. Do the same with the other leg. Movements should be continuous and rather fast. (See Figure 6.)

Figure 6

Starting from an erect position, bend over, placing hands on floor, bending knees so that you are in a squatting position. Throw right leg behind you so that weight is supported on hands and toes of other foot. Bring leg toward chin. Bring leg back to first position and stand erect. Do exercise with other leg.

Stand erect. Kick right leg as high as it will go. Lower. Repeat exercise with other leg.

Do a bicycle roll. Start by lying on your back, then using your hands to prop your hips, raising legs high, until you're balanced into position. Now pretend that you're riding a bike, moving legs faster and faster.

Lie on left side, left knee bent, torso raised off floor. Rest on left elbow with hands on floor in front of you. Raise right leg high without bending. Rotate it outward, toe pointed toward ceiling. Change sides after doing this 5 times and repeat exercise.

FOR THE ANKLES

Sitting on a straight chair with legs out in front of you, bend foot with toes toward you. Now point toes away from body. Put one foot on floor. Leave other foot outstretched and rotate from the ankle to the right, then to the left. Do same exercise with other leg, reversing position.

Sit on floor and cross legs at knee. Pointing toe, make circles with your ankle starting with tiny ones and then moving to larger circles, first to one side and then to the other. Switch legs and repeat.

Stand with heels on a book. (A telephone book will do.) Body should be erect with hands clasped behind neck, weight balanced on heels. Lower toes to floor, stretching muscles of ankle and instep. Raise toes to original position.

Walk across the room on your toes, keeping your body straight.

Stand erect. Raise up on toes. Lower to floor.

FOR THE CALVES

Stand grasping the back of a straight chair. Bend both knees about a third of the way. Keep right knee bent. Extend left leg back, straightening the knee, and place ball of the foot on the floor (foot faces forward). Bounce left heel toward floor. Change leg and bounce right heel.

Stand with feet together, arms straight ahead. Keep back erect, heels down. Bend knees until you feel strong pull in thighs. Clasp hands behind neck and count to three. Arms extended, continue knee-bend, heels down. Bend from hips, but don't slump forward. Stand. Keep back erect. Let the legs do the work.

FOR THE BUST

Stand erect. Place arms at sides, out from shoulders. Make circles backward, starting with small circles and gradually making large circles. Now do circles forward.

Stand erect, feet together, arms at sides. Bend arms and raise so that elbows are at shoulder level, hands clenched in fists against the chest. Rotate elbows in as large a circle as possible.

Stand erect with tennis racket in right hand, feet about 15 inches apart. Raise racket, swinging it past right ankle to rear and up above head at arm's length, then to floor. Shift to left hand and swing.

Lie flat on stomach (you may use a pillow if you wish) with hands clasped behind you. Lift head and torso off floor, pull arms up in back. Then, as in swimming, bend elbows, bringing arms forward close to chest. Straighten arms as they go in front of you. To complete stroke, pull arms back in wide arc as if you were really swimming. Keep torso lifted throughout exercise.

Use a rolling pin (or any lightweight rod of similar size). Place legs apart and bend forward, holding rolling pin behind your body. Pull pin as high as you can behind you.

Stand with legs apart, back straight and head erect. Lift arms to chest level and press palm of one hand against the other. With your right palm, push the left arm back slowly about a foot. Now reverse and push right arm back with left. The arm being pushed back should resist fairly strenuously, so that you feel a tension in the chest area.

FOR THE BACK

Stand with feet together, hands on hips. Bend forward as far as possible, keeping knees straight. Now swing backward as far as you can go and still keep your balance. Inhale as you swing forward and exhale as you go backward.

Get down on your hands and knees. Take a deep breath and relax. Let head hang down. Pull stomach in and curve back upward. Now arch back and raise head up. Relax. Repeat 5 times. (See Figures 7a and 7b.)

Figure 7a

Figure 7b

Sit Indian style, clasp ankles from underneath. Bend head forward as far as you can go, trying to touch ground. (See Figure 8.)

Figure 8

Lie flat on stomach, hands clasped behind head with toes pointed. Slowly lift head, shoulders, elbows and legs off floor. Return to original position. Don't strain too much the first few times. Gradually try to reach higher.

FOR THE FACE

Shut eyes and contract eyebrows to try to make them meet. Raise eyelids and brows. Your ears will move up and down. Squint and tense tightly and shut eyes alternately. Depress brows, first one side and then the other.

Pucker mouth and resist strongly by pulling sides of mouth together by sucking in. Clench teeth, smile broadly and pull cheeks back while tensing. Open mouth as wide as you can and pull teeth together slowly and tightly. With tension, move lower jaw side to side alternately. Extend as much to the rear as possible. Close lips tightly and force air into each cheek. Relax.

Throw head back and open mouth. Pull closed with tension as you do. This will help eliminate a double chin.

FOR THE SHOULDERS

Sit tailor-fashion with back straight, hands resting on thighs. Shrug first one shoulder and then the other, bringing shoulders up to ears. Make circles with each shoulder, back to front and front to back.

14

Ways to Appear Slimmer
Until You Reach Your Goal

Every woman wants to look as attractive as she can, no matter how much she weighs. There is no reason to wait until you've lost all your excess pounds. You can start to look better right away. We're going to attempt to take your mind off snacking and overeating by having you concentrate on making yourself into a more beautiful person. Make note of the fact that I said "more beautiful," because you already are a beautiful person. Every human being that God created is beautiful.

YOUR NATURAL BEAUTY

Many women, whether overweight or otherwise, simply do not know what to do with the natural beauty they possess. They may think of themselves as plain and unattractive and so do nothing about accentuating their good points. Also, the more overweight they become, the less beauty they can see in themselves, so they lack the motivation they need to improve their looks. You, too, have probably experienced that helpless feeling when you looked into your full-length mirror and saw that 40 or 50 extra pounds on your body transformed you into an older, matronly-looking woman. It's no wonder that beauty seems to be so unattainable. We have to turn your thinking around—that is, brainwash you into believing that you do have the makings of a beautiful woman, so that by the time you lose those unwanted pounds, you will truly be beautiful. In the interim, let's camouflage as many undesirable points as you can detect and play up whatever good points you possess.

Stop right now and make a list of all your good qualities. When you last had a compliment from a friend, what was it that was praised? Your long lashes? The color of your eyes? Your shiny hair? Or was it something about your personality? Your good sense of humor? Your patience? Your ability to be a good listener? The truly beautiful woman is beautiful inside as well as outside. Make that list and keep it, adding to it as you go on with your diet and lose those unwanted pounds. You will actually be able to see your progress toward becoming a more lovely woman. As we go along, try to think of ways in which you can accentuate your good points and hide or do away with the bad ones.

SKIN CARE AND THE BATH

Let's start with your skin and how to care for it. A bath or shower is essential each day, not only for personal cleanliness, but also to keep your pores unclogged. It's much easier to avoid blackheads than to get rid of them. A clean appearance is always more beautiful, making you nice to be around.

Your bathtime can be your relaxing time of the day. The water should be pleasantly warm, but not too hot. Experiment with various bath oils or bubble baths to see which you will choose to use permanently—the one that not only makes you feel good, but is also kind to your skin. Underarms and legs will be easier to shave after soaking in your bath, so this is a good time to take care of that necessity. It's time to get out of the tub when the water starts to feel too cool. Don't stay in so long that your skin starts to shrivel. Follow your bath with a shower, starting with warm water and ending with cooler or cold water to close your pores.

Pat your body dry with a large fluffy bath towel and then rub a body moisturizer all over until it is absorbed into your skin. Apply an anti-perspirant and your favorite cologne.

USING COLOGNE

Cologne or toilet water has a lighter scent and can be applied more freely all over the body than perfume. It will make you feel sensuously kissable all over. Try out new fragrances even if you think you are content with your present one. Next time you are at a perfume counter, apply two new fragrances, using the tester bottle, one to each arm or wrist. Rub it into your skin and then take a sniff. You may think you know whether you like it or not right away, but wait until later in the day to decide. Sniff it an hour later and see how the scent has lingered and if it still smells the same, or is somehow different and/or better. Be sure to make a note of what brands you have tested so that you can try different ones each time. If you think you like one of the brands you've tested, buy the smallest size available, use it and see if you get any compliments when you wear it. Wearing a fragrance is a terrific morale booster for any woman. I feel naked if I don't have cologne on, even when I'm not going to be around anyone else. Smelling good and being aware of it myself makes me feel more feminine and I like feeling that way.

THE MANICURE

Once a week you should give yourself a manicure and a pedicure even if you think your hands are ugly and your nails are too short. You may find that if you start paying attention to them, they will start looking better each week. If you bite your nails, stop it immediately. You must also stop using your nails as if they were tools. Naturally, your nails are going to keep breaking if you use them to pry, scrape or even scratch.

While you are still in your bath, try to remember to push back your cuticles with an orange stick. It's the best time to do it, while your skin is most pliable.

Take off all old nail polish with a Q-tip dipped in polish remover. Use an orange stick with a small piece of cotton on the end and, using the polish remover, carefully clean the underside of the nail. Trim off any hangnails with cuticle cutters, being careful not to cut the cuticle. You may want to soak your hands and nails in lotion or warm olive oil now if they appear to be dry. Use metal nail clippers to cut your nails to the length you want and then use an emery board to shape the tip. Never file the lower sides of the nails and always use the emery board in one direction when shaping because going against the grain can cause cracking or leave weak spots. Make sure all rough areas are gone before applying polish. After you finish filing, wipe off all the fine dust with a damp tissue so that it doesn't lump together and give your nails a grainy look.

For the base coat, use a clear polish with an oil base. Do the lower part of the nail first, making sure to cover the edges. Cover the top of the nail with long, even strokes. Give adequate time for the nails to dry thoroughly and then apply a second coat. Now apply the actual nail polish, using two coats. Finish with one coat of colorless sealer. If your nails are extremely short you should stay away from bright or dark red shades, keeping more to rose and pink hues. If you don't care to wear color at all on your nails, then the base coat plus a colorless sealer coat will be sufficient to make you appear well groomed.

THE PEDICURE

If you are doing your pedicure at some time other than right after your bath, you may want to soak your feet in a basin of warm sudsy water. This will relax you, loosen any dirt under the nails and soften the cuticles. Clean the nails with cotton on the end of an orange stick. Then use the orange stick to push back the cuticle. Trim the nails with a metal nail clipper and shape with an emery board. When filing, go straight across the nail. Do not try to shape nails into a point, as cutting or filing from the sides can cause ingrown toenails. You may want to use this opportunity to apply a foot cream or some kind of moisturizing lotion to your feet, massaging them to relieve tension.

Before applying polish, use a tissue to remove all traces of cream on the nails themselves. Apply two coats of base polish, two coats of colored polish, and finish with one coat of sealer. You should of course match the color of polish with the color on your fingernails. Allow at least an hour to do both the manicure and the pedicure.

HAIR CARE

Beautiful hair has been a symbol of feminine beauty throughout history. Hair makes a frame for your face and that frame can make you seem taller or shorter, or even thinner or fatter than you are. Hair that is long as well as flat on top will tend to make you look shorter. Most women, unless they are over 5'10" tall, will not want to appear shorter, for tallness is one of the professional model's best qualities. Long hair which is worn close to the face may also make you seem heavier than you are, but if you really know you look your best in long hair (or if you keep it long because your man prefers it that way), continue wearing it the way you feel most comfortable.

A short hairstyle makes your neck look longer and the overall appearance of your total body more slender, and it is becoming to both young and old. Whatever style you choose, pick one that is easy to manage as well as becoming. You don't want to be spending hours each week in a beauty salon just because you can't set your own hair. Don't pick a style that is too short or mannish-looking as this will accentuate your heaviness as well as take away from your femininity.

Bangs can be used in a variety of ways with varying results, depending on whether they are straight or curly, parted on the side or with no part, thick or thin. If your ears are large or if they protrude, it is best to choose a hairstyle that covers at least the tops of them to minimize their size.

CHANGING YOUR HAIR COLOR

You may feel like changing the color of your hair while you are dieting to give you a little lift. If you've always wondered why they say that "blondes have more fun," now is the time to find out. If you've always thought your hair had a touch of auburn in it, why not try a more daring shade of red and see if it wears well on you. Now's the time to experiment and take chances on a new look for yourself. Do everything you can to make losing weight a fun time in your life.

SHAMPOOING

More important than the length or color of your hair is how clean and healthy it is. You should shampoo your hair once or twice a week if it is oily. Shampoos can be selected in normal, dry and oily formulas in the same brand.

Wet your hair and scalp thoroughly with warm water. Apply enough shampoo to work up a thick lather. Massage your scalp as you wash your hair. Place your thumbs close together at the back of your head and rest the fingertips on the top of your head. Being careful not to scratch your scalp with your nails or rough treatment, rotate each finger in a circle until you feel a tingly sensation in that area. Change the position of your fingers and rotate them until you have treated your whole scalp to this stimulating massage.

Rinse the hair and then shampoo again. Rinse with warm water until all shampoo is gone. Finish with a creme rinse to help make the hair more manageable and easier to comb out the tangles. To add luster to your hair you can use a lemon or vinegar rinse that you make yourself. Use the strained juice of two lemons in a bowlful of warm water or a tablespoon of vinegar to a quart of water. If you have extremely dry hair, you can add a drop of baby oil to the final rinse water.

Don't ever use dry shampoo unless you really must. It has a tendency to leave your hair dull and it is hard to remove the powdery substance left behind on your hair.

The hair should be brushed at least once every day. Bend your head over in front of you and brush all your hair forward. Now brush in the opposite direction as you straighten up. Brushing stimulates the scalp and actually makes the hair stronger as well as shinier-looking.

YOUR FACE

Always apply your makeup to a clean face. You don't need fancy creams—just good old-fashioned soap and water will do. After drying your face, you may want to apply a skin moisturizer if you have dry skin, or an astringent lotion if your skin is oily. Over the moisturizer apply a thin coat of foundation with your fingertips. Blend cream or liquid rouge onto the cheeks. Suck in your cheeks to see where the lower line of shading should go. To avoid a shiny face, dust with powder.

Use the fingertips to apply eye shadow on each lid. Use natural tones such as browns, grays or blue-grays. Keep away from bright blues, greens and metallic shades. You may want to line the eye at the base of the upper lashes. Try to blend the liner into the eye shadow so that the makeup job is not so obvious. Make sure you've plucked out all the straggly hairs between your eyebrows and below the natural brow arch. If your brows are very light, you may want to darken them with a light brown or medium brown eyebrow pencil. Avoid black pencil unless your hair is actually black. Brush mascara onto the lashes in the direction in which they grow. Brown mascara is good for light brown-haired or blonde women and black mascara is for dark-haired or dark-complected women.

Lipstick should be applied following the natural lipline. Brunettes can use the darker, brighter red shades, but women with lighter hair should try to stick to pinks or light reds. Blot twice with a tissue, first biting it and then placing it over the lips as if kissing the tissue. This way the excess will come off on the tissue instead of on the things you touch with your lips. Learn to use a lip brush for a really professional look.

If you have oily skin, instead of liquid or cream foundation you may wish to use a product called pancake makeup, which is put out by Max Factor. It's applied to the face using a damp sponge. Many models use it when they are having photographs made because it covers most common skin blemishes and makes the skin appear flawless. With this makeup you'll use powdered rouge or blusher put on with a dry brush, and dry eye shadow applied with a sponge-tipped applicator. You won't need powder, as the pancake dries to a matte finish.

Many women who think of themselves as plain and even unattractive are that way because they have never explored using makeup to make themselves look better. They have the mistaken impression that, if you have natural beauty, you can and should go around with no makeup. They are afraid to use makeup for fear that it will make them look hard or grotesque. What they don't realize, and what few people do, is that professional models who look as if they aren't wearing any makeup may actually have as much makeup on as those who appear "made up." It takes incredible skill and practice to make it look like you're not wearing any makeup at all. Those models were not born with that knowledge. They learned it by practicing the application of makeup, trying new cosmetic products, experimenting with new colors and color combinations until they found what was just right for them. This can really be a lot of fun and I want you to start trying out different ways of making up your face until you find out what's right for you. When your face looks good and your hair looks good, it draws attention away from your figure problems, and that's what you want to do while you're still in the process of losing weight.

CLOTHES

Now let's look over your wardrobe. Certain clothes can make you look slimmer or appear heavier. The same goes for the colors you wear. You are out to create an illusion of beauty, doing the most with what you have to work with.

Every woman loves clothes, but you have to take into consideration several things when making your selection:

- *Where you live*. Casual clothes that are acceptable in Miami or another resort city may not be suitable for Chicago or New York. You want to appear as well-dressed as you can and still stay within your budget. Also, you want to use what you already have without buying new clothes if you can help it, because after you lose your weight, you'll want to give all your "fat" clothes away to some charitable institution. You'll never want to see them again to remind you that you once were "that fat." Another reason you won't want to keep your "fat" clothes is because you may be tempted to slide back into bad habits and put the weight back on, if you know there is something hanging in your closet to wear.

- *The type of activities you are usually involved in*. If you are a mother and homemaker who seldom goes out to parties, you will certainly need a different wardrobe than a college student, a businesswoman or a gay divorcee. Your leisure clothes, even if you are only hanging around the house or your apartment, should be something nicer than your old, out-of-fashion clothes or shoes. You need to look as nice as you can at all times, if only for your own morale.

High fashion magazines don't always provide the help you're looking for because, for one thing, they show how the latest fashions look on extremely tall, thin models. It's hard for an overweight person to visualize herself in a new fashion in order to decide if she may be able to wear it. Furthermore, high fashion changes quickly and unless you have unlimited financial resources, you'll find that you can't keep up with it even if you talk yourself into believing that you can wear one of the latest styles.

If you're not sure what to wear to appear well-dressed, study what some of the prominent women in your own community wear and copy some of their ideas, adapting them as you must to try to make you look more slender.

While you are overweight, make sure that your clothing does not fit you too snugly, since this will only make your problem more apparent. Don't wear clothing that is much too large for you either, for that can make you seem bigger than you really are. Never wear short-sleeved dresses or dresses without any sleeves. High collars and wide belts are also to be avoided. Always wear high heels and keep your hemlines below the knees, but not as far down as your ankles.

Keep away from a cute or coy look with ruffles, bows and ribbons. If you wear stripes, they should be vertical and all prints should be small. Plain colors in dark shades are preferable to any kind of print. Colors such as black, charcoal, dark brown, dark green, maroon and navy blue should make up most of your wardrobe.

When wearing a jacket or vest with a dress, skirt or slacks, be sure the jacket or vest comes down over the seat for the best slimming effect. A good "uniform" for the overweight woman is a plain-colored princess-style dress without a belt topped by a contrasting vest in a darker shade of the same color. In cooler weather, a jacket can be utilized instead of the vest. Never use a printed or lighter-colored vest or jacket, because this will defeat your purpose. Using this suggestion, you can even wear taboo colors such as white and all the pastels. Visualize yourself in a white dress with a V-neck, a navy blue jacket and a red scarf around your neck. White or gold jewelry can be used for accessories. You'll appear well-dressed at any daytime function in this outfit.

In choosing what colors to wear, consider the color of your hair as a guide, rather than what colors you think you like. What you like may not look particularly good on you. Blondes can wear just about any color they choose. Redheads can use black, brown, navy, green or maroon as their basic dark color. Brunettes should steer clear of black, navy and maroon, selecting instead browns and greens. Black-haired brunettes may use black, navy, green or maroon, but avoid the browns. If you have gray hair, you'll want to stay away from browns, too, but you can wear the other colors I've mentioned. The colors I've suggested are the ones you will wear in the darkest hues as an overall color when wearing only one color, or as your outer color (for jacket or vest) when wearing two colors, or two shades of the same color.

Here are some of the color combinations you can try:

With black: white, yellow, pink, pale blue, pale green, beige, gray.

With navy: white, pale blue, pale yellow, peach. (Red may be used only as an accent color, but not as a second color, since it attracts too much attention to your body.)

With brown: any other lighter shades of brown, pink, pale green, peach, white, yellow.

With maroon: white, pink, pale blue, gray.

If you have a formal occasion coming up and you feel you look too heavy in your long dress, have a long, contrasting vest made for it to disguise any bulges you may have in your waistline. I shouldn't need to say this, but your formal should have long sleeves. If it doesn't, then have a contrasting "coat" made to go over your formal instead of the vest. The "coat" can be made of lace or semi-sheer material. Black velvet looks elegant as a vest for formal occasions. You can trim it with rhinestone buttons.

In choosing a coat to wear for cold weather, select a dark color. It should be full length with no waistline. A princess line would be more flattering than a straight box line.

If you like to wear skirts and blouses, choose blouses that are worn over the skirt rather than tucked in. Never wear a skirt that is gathered at the waistline. The skirt should be fitted at the waistline and hips and flare out to a full skirt for the best slenderizing effect. Two-piece dresses should break at the hipline and not at the waist.

Go through your closet and see what acceptable outfits you already have. You may want to invest in a new jacket to match a favorite dress. If you sew you can make yourself some vests in a variety of colors to create new outfits from your present wardrobe. They are easy and inexpensive to make.

15

The Charming New You
and How to Stay That Way

There are hundreds of books telling you how to lose weight, but very few that even touch on the subject of how to maintain that ideal weight once you've reached it. It isn't going to happen by itself. *You* have to make it happen. The day you look down at the numbers on your bathroom scale and see that they are the ones you've been dreaming of is one of the most crucial days of your diet. At first you may have a feeling of disbelief. After you've been fat for so long it's hard to believe that you have finally reached your goal. It's too good to be true! Many ex-"fatties" think of themselves as overweight even when they lose those extra pounds. They find it almost impossible to think of themselves as normal. This is a common reaction.

THE RIGHT WAY TO CELEBRATE

When you realize that it is really true, that you *are* at the weight you want to be, you will feel like celebrating immediately. Fine. Just don't celebrate by eating anything. If you do, you'll surely eat all the wrong things and find yourself overweight again by tomorrow.

Psychologically, this day is very important because, if you start to slip backwards after reaching your goal, it can make you so depressed that you may fall into old eating patterns and quickly put on a lot of weight in only a matter of days. I hope I can get through to you that you can never, and I mean never, eat the way you used to when you put on all those excess pounds. If you do, it is a fact that you will get fat again. There is no avoiding it. After what you've been through to lose all your excess weight, I'm sure you don't want to put yourself in the position of having to do it again. Most people *won't* do it again; they'll just let themselves go and say, "What's the use? I was meant to be fat."

The day you reach your desired weight, you have to make a promise to yourself that you will keep that weight for the rest of your life, no matter what steps you have to take to do it. You have to want this more than anything else so that you will have the willpower to succeed and keep that promise.

The biggest problem facing you is how to find out how much you can safely eat without putting on any added pounds. The only way you can do this accurately is to keep a record of everything you eat from now on just as you did when you were on the 600 calorie diet. We know that you lose weight when you only eat 600 calories, so to maintain your present weight you will have to eat more than that. Start by adding 300 more calories per day for the next three days and see what happens when you weigh yourself each day. You'll then be eating 900 calories per day, which is still a reducing diet for most people. If your weight stays the same, stay on the 900 calorie plan for 3 more days. If you find that you are gaining a fraction of a pound, cut back to 800 calories for 3 days. If you see that you are losing weight by eating 900 calories, add 300 more calories each day, making a total of 1200 calories. After you work yourself up to 1200 calories, stay on this diet for one week and see what happens. If you find that you are losing some weight after the end of the first week, add 100 calories per day to your diet. Be sure to weigh yourself every day. It is very important that you watch your calorie count and be accurate about the amounts so that you can determine just how much you can eat without gaining weight. I know I'm asking you to do a most tedious task, but believe me, it will be worth it. You will know exactly where you stand when it comes to eating. You'll be able to eat almost anything you want to eat in the future as long as you use portions which fit into your allowed calorie count for the day. Your calorie count will be strictly for you, based on your life, how you work and how you play.

While you are trying to maintain your weight, it is a good idea to stick to simple foods that will make counting your calories easier.

Here is a list of the things you may *not* eat while trying to keep your weight stable:

TV dinners	Chili con carne
Chicken croquettes	Pizza
Pot pies	Spaghetti and meatballs
Creamed anything	Sausage
Baked beans	Gravy
Lamb	Fried oysters
Pork	French fried potatoes
Ham	French fried onion rings
Ravioli	Macaroni and cheese
Lasagna	Breaded veal cutlet
Pancakes	Sandwiches

Brownies	Danish pastry
Banana splits	Cookies
Blintzes	Pies
Cakes	Eclairs
Candy (except hard)	Napoleons
Cheesecake	Puddings
Cream puffs	Jelly rolls
Cupcakes	Parfaits
Donuts	Petit fours
Ice cream	Turnovers
Ice milk	Tarts
Frozen custard	Gingerbread
Sherbet	Sweet rolls
Strudel	Sodas
Sundaes	Strawberry shortcake
Glazed fruit	Whipped cream

Whole milk	Popovers
Salad oil	Cream
Potato chips or other similar snacks	Salad dressings
	Peanut butter
Jams, preserves and marmalade	Cornbread

After you've determined how many calories you can allow yourself each day, and you've been able to maintain your weight for at least one month, you can add any of these foods in moderate amounts to put variety into your lifetime diet plan.

REWARDING YOURSELF

Now that you're slender, most of the clothes in your closet will be too big for you. Reward yourself with something new, depending on what you can afford. Very few women will be able to go out and choose a whole new wardrobe, but any woman can allow herself at least one new outfit. Shop for a form-fitting style with a definite waistline, no boxy styles, no vests or jackets. Pick yourself up by selecting a color you haven't been able to wear before. You'll feel like an entirely new woman.

Have your photograph made wearing your new "thin" outfit. You could have a friend take it with a Polaroid or Instamatic, but I believe you've earned the right to have a professional photographer do it. After all, it's a very special occasion. Look in the yellow pages of the telephone directory and see which photographers specialize in glamour photography; don't just hire *any* portrait photographer. If the ads don't say, "We specialize in glamour photography," then look to see if they say something like, "Model's composites our specialty," or, "Theatrical Photos." These photographers will be able to make you look your best because they are used to working with professional models and entertainers who must look as good as or better than they really are, for their photographs are used to get them employment. Try to find out over the phone just how much they charge and how many poses they will take for you to choose from. You can let them know that you are not a professional model, but you'd like to look your prettiest because you've just lost some weight. Since most of us look better later in the day when we've been up and around for a while, than we do in the morning when we first get up, make sure to make your appointment with the photographer in the afternoon.

This photograph will be a great morale booster and a constant reminder of how you want to look from now on. You'll want a copy not only for yourself, but also for your boyfriend or your husband. Put the photograph where you can see and admire it every day.

Another photograph you should have taken at this time is one in which you are wearing either a bathing suit or a leotard. Use a felt-tip pen and write across the top of it the date when it was taken and how much you weighed at that time. This photograph should be posted right inside your closet door, unless it's so fantastically good that you want to display it in the living room for all to see. You could have this photo made at the same time as you are being photographed in your new outfit. The photographer, of course, will charge you extra for any costume changes, so if you cannot afford to have two different photographs made, let a friend do it for you with a Polaroid or Instamatic camera. Make sure that your face is not shiny when you have your pictures taken, since that makes the light bounce around on your face and do strange things to it. Use a matte-finish makeup, such as Max Factor's pancake makeup, or pat powder over any other kind of makeup base.

LETTING OTHERS SEE YOU

Now that you have a new body and a new outfit, you should start going out more. Socialize and be seen more. After all, now you are someone who is nice to look at.

Another bonus in having a slender body is that it makes you look younger than you are, or at least younger than you used to look when you were heavy. Try to erase your age from your memory. Be the age you want to be. From now on, when you look into your mirror, say to yourself, "It's true. I'm getting prettier every day." Smile as you say it. In fact, start concentrating on smiling as often as you can throughout your day. Frowns and bored or worried looks can make you look tired. When you look tired, you look older. By smiling more often, you'll not only appear prettier to those around you, you'll also make them happier.

Now that you'll be going out more often, you're probably wondering what you can do to make yourself more popular or what you can do to improve your personality.

First of all, when preparing to go out to a party or other special occasion, make sure that your grooming is as correct as you can make it. You don't want to be worried about a slip that might start showing because it was the wrong length, or whether you might have bad breath because you didn't floss your teeth after eating a steak at dinner. Put yourself together so confidently that you won't even have to think once about how you will come across to other people. You must believe that you are beautiful, so that you will have time to concentrate on other people instead of on yourself.

Have you ever noticed how much prettier someone is when they are first in love? It gives them confidence in themselves to know that someone finds them charming and irresistible. Because they *feel* prettier, they actually *look* prettier. This is the kind of confidence you will need so that you can develop your personality and popularity.

MAKING YOURSELF GOOD COMPANY

People are happier with you and like you more if they are comfortable in your company. If you have a habit of blurting out things which tend to upset people, or even using mannerisms which irritate others, you will find that people will go to any lengths to avoid you. It's difficult to see your own faults, but you must try if you are to succeed in being a better person.

Ask questions so that it gives the other person a chance to open up to you and make his feelings known first. This way you'll know how to steer the conversation so that it can be pleasant and lead to a friendly relationship.

When you say things that the other person wants to hear, you immediately become interesting to him. Just put the shoe on the other foot for a moment. What would you think of a person you had just met who asked questions about your hobby and then listened attentively while you rambled on, taking pleasure in talking about a subject that pleased you? You'd naturally think that the other person was intelligent, fascinating and, in general, had a good personality. Besides that, you'd probably rate them as attractive if someone later asked you what you had thought of that person.

So, if you want someone that you've just met to think well of you, try to remove the pronoun "I" from your conversation if you can. Direct your attention to the other person, looking him straight in the eyes and being a good, undistracted listener when he is talking. Interrupt only when the right spot comes up to ask a question so that he can elaborate even more on his favorite subject. Eventually he will throw some questions back at you, so be prepared for this and the conversation will run along on a smooth course.

Try to compliment sincerely at least one person every day. With every person that you meet, try to find something worthwhile about him or her that you can honestly use as a basis for a compliment.

Don't be afraid to pay another person a compliment. It may be the one thing that makes their day. Everyone loves a compliment, even when they act embarrassed, as if they don't deserve it. You and your compliment will be remembered long after the conversation is over, and you'll be remembered well.

I've advised you to smile a lot when you come into contact with other people, but many times you cannot smile without looking disinterested. Look at yourself in the mirror and try to train your face to assume a pleasant expression that you can use while listening to someone talk. There is no need to look grim when someone is discussing a serious subject. Keep the corners of your mouth turned up, not down. When the corners turn down, it makes you look older. Keep a sparkle in your eyes, so that you almost glow. The glow you see outside comes from within. If you sincerely try to be interested in the other person, you'll come across that way.

If you have trouble making entrances, say at a large cocktail party, try this method. Just after entering the room, position yourself to one side of the doorway, poising yourself with your head held high, looking around (keep the pleasant expression on your face) as if you are looking for a certain someone. If you see someone you know, you can head for that group and feel at home right away. If you look all around and see no one you know, not even your hostess, pick out a small group and walk directly over and speak to the man whose back is toward you. You can touch him on the shoulder or just say, "Hi!" When he turns to look at who is there, look surprised and say, "Oh, I'm sorry. From the back you looked just like Joe Stevens. Do you know Joe?" From there on, you have someone to talk to whether they know who Joe is or not.

The sound of your voice is very important when you talk with people. It can make you seem young or old, beautiful or unattractive. Read a paragraph or two of a book or newspaper into a tape recorder, play it back and listen to how you sound. If you don't like what you hear, other people won't, either. See if you can pinpoint your trouble spots and do something about them.

An excellent way to practice improving your voice is to read aloud once a day to another person. Try reading the Bible with someone you love, taking turns each day. If you aren't religiously inclined, enjoy a novel with someone else. This might be a good time to offer your reading services to a nursing home or hospital.

The end result of this book is to make you into a more interesting, attractive woman. The woman who is confident of her charm and beauty has more fun in life than the woman who is unsure of herself and lacks concern about her physical appearance. Why forsake all the good times that may just be waiting for you to partake of them? Doors open more easily for the charming woman. Her easy-going personality makes her desirable for parties, companionship and marriage. We don't live in a vacuum. We need the acceptance of the world around us. We need to feel wanted and loved. We have to reach out and give of ourselves to attain this. No one is going to seek us out of our dark caves and offer it to us. Make the most of what you have, accentuating all of your positive qualities and hiding or eliminating entirely the negative things. Remember, you *are* a new woman now. The old woman, who was matronly-looking, fat, tired, and disinterested in living, is gone forever. You can erase her memory now and replace it with the exciting new you.

SO NOW YOU WANT TO BE A MODEL!

Haven't you ever had a secret desire to be a professional model? I'm sure every girl has, but many things stop the average girl from realizing her fantasy. Not every girl is qualified to become a professional model, but even those who are may lack the necessary confidence in themselves. Many girls, even if they are quite attractive, never feel that they are beautiful enough to become models, so they don't even try.

Your main drawback was probably your excess weight, but now that you have a new slender body and a new outlook on life, you owe it to yourself to find out if you can be a model. You'll never know if you don't try, and now, when you know you look your very best, is a good time to try.

Let me briefly clarify what it means to be a professional model these days. Professional, of course, means that you are paid for what you do, whether you are just starting out and making $10.00 an hour or you are a top model grossing $100,000 or $200,000 per year. You may never make it to the top bracket; few do, but if you are worth anything at all as a model, you will not stay in the $10.00 per hour range for long. Most models fluctuate between the $40.00 an hour and $75.00 an hour bracket.

You don't have to take a modeling course in order to be a model. If you can afford to, great; it's icing on the cake. But I'm going to tell you how to be a model without going to the extra expense of taking costly modeling lessons. These days, how you look is more important than how you walk. Your type, not how well you function on a fashion show runway, is what counts.

Modeling is not something that you work at from 9 to 5 each day with Saturday and Sunday off. Modeling can take place at almost any time of the day or night and you may work for 30 minutes on one job and 12 hours on another.

There are all kinds of people who are called models. Babies, children, teens, women and men from 20 to 60. It used to be that all models were 5'8" and over, bone skinny and ultra high fashion in looks. With the popularity of television and the need for all types of people to appear in TV commercials came the acceptance of everyday people to be used as models. Instead of sneaking into the kitchen for a snack when the commercials come on, watch them and notice the variety of people who appear. If you hadn't made up your mind yet about trying to become a model, you will then. The first thing you'll say to yourself is, "I can do that. And I look as good as she does or better."

It isn't that easy to get started, but it can be easier if you know something about how to go about it. What you must understand is that modeling is not something that you play with. Modeling is a serious profession and, unless you treat it that way, you won't go far. In fact, you won't go anywhere.

Sherry L., a striking honey blonde with enormous eyes and pouting lips, came to me looking for modeling work. It was obvious from the way she talked and acted that everyone she knew had told her she should be a model. I asked her if she had any pictures to show me of herself. She said, "No, I didn't think I needed any if you could see me in person." I patiently explained to her that there was no way I could tell her at that moment whether I could use her or not. I had to see photographs. She either had to bring some to me and leave one for my file or she would have to call and make an appointment with me for another day when I was not so busy and I would make some test shots of her.

"Sherry," I said, "you're a very pretty girl, but you will never make it as a model if you continue to conduct yourself in an unprofessional way. All of the people who hire models are professional people and they don't have time to play games. Their time is valuable. The first thing you must have to become a model is a portfolio of photographs of yourself at your best. You show these when you come for your interview. Then, if possible, have a composite of several photos on one sheet that you can leave with the client. Why photographs? Because, Sherry, you are not the only girl I will look at and interview today. (And it's the same with other people who have to interview models.) At the end of the day when I have collected photographs of most of the girls who come in looking for work and I have to make a selection of two or three girls, it is relatively simple when I have a photo to look at to remind me of what the girl looked like in person. If you don't have a photo with your employment application, my mind may be a blur as to what your features actually looked like. Then, too, you may have looked all right in person but you may not photograph well. You will just not be considered for a modeling job if you don't have a photograph to represent you, no matter how nice the interviewer may seem. We can't take the chance. Another thing: I, the photographer, may not do the selecting. My client may leave it up to me to spend my time looking at girls, interviewing them and collecting their photos, and then I may turn the photos over to him to make the final selection. Can you imagine how stupid I would look handing him an application without a photo, while I tried to remember what you looked like and tried to describe you to him? There is no way you will get any professional modeling jobs without showing pictures of yourself. So, Sherry, your career in modeling is up to you. You can be what you want to be, but you have to do it in the accepted professional way."

I ran into Sherry about 10 months later while doing a photography job for a furniture manufacturer. The client had selected his own models and I had no idea of whom they would be. Sherry walked over when she recognized me and said, "I took your advice; want to see my portfolio?" I answered, "Sherry, how good to see you and how well you look! You've changed your hair and your makeup somewhat, but I still knew it was you. Of course I want to look at your portfolio." I couldn't believe it. Her portfolio contained so many photographs taken by so many different photographers that she had a hard time getting the zipper closed after I was through looking at it. She was well on her way to becoming a successful professional model then, and the last I heard was that she is working in New York now and I'm hoping to get a prosperous report from her soon.

I get a lot of pleasure out of knowing what happens to a girl and her career after she models for me. I'm so proud when they do well and I can say, "I knew them when..."

So, your first step if you want to become a professional model is to find a photographer who specializes in photographing models, preferably one who is experienced in glamour as well as high fashion photography. A high fashion photographer will concentrate on making the clothes look good, but a glamour photographer will concentrate on you, making the very best of the good features you have.

If you don't have much money to spend on your new career, the very basic minimum for photography is an 8″ by 10″ black and white glossy head shot (portrait) of yourself, unretouched. Most photographers take at least 12 poses, of which you ought to be able to pick out one that is best. You take this one 8″ by 10″ print to a place that specializes in making inexpensive multiple copies and order at least 100 copies. In this quantity, they should cost about 20¢-25¢ each.

If you do have some money to donate to the cause, then have a model's composite made. The photographer will take 36 or more poses of you wearing various outfits. You select four or six of the best ones and he arranges them on an 8″ by 10″ sheet. Then you take this arrangement of photos to your multiple printer and have 100 copies made. Many models have 1000 copies made, but when you have 500 or more copies to be made it is cheaper and just as acceptable to have them printed on paper stock by a lithographer or offset printer. The outfits you might wear for a composite are: dressy dress, suit, slack set, blue jeans and shirt, long dress, tennis outfit, bathing suit.

The next professional step, after you have your photographs made and ready to show the world, is to find an agent. For a list of agents to call, consult the yellow pages of the telephone book under the heading of Modeling Agencies. You have to realize when you call these people that they don't need you; *you* need them! Here is the best way to call for an appointment: "Hello, I'm Laurie Loveable. Could you tell me when I could come in and show you my photographs?"

Many agents will only look at new talent one day a week. If that is the situation, don't ask them to change their schedule for you.

Remember, you need them; they don't need you. If an agent finds work for you, he will charge 10 or 15 percent of the amount you are paid. There is no fee to register with a legitimate agency. If they ask for a fee, walk out the door and try a different agent.

An agent may ask you for 10 to 20 photographs or composites to put in their file. One will go into their permanent file and the others will be put in a file with your name on it, or you may be filed as to your type. This is so that when a client comes in looking for a certain kind of model, he can look through the master file and, when he comes across a girl he thinks he might like to hire, he asks the agency for a copy of her photo or composite to take with him to either show someone else who has to help make the decision or to have the photos with him at his place of business where he can take his time to go over them and decide which model to use. These photos are usually kept by the person who takes them, so an agency must have enough copies on hand to service a number of clients who may choose you as a "semi-finalist."

When you become popular, you may find that an agent wants to sign you to an exclusive contract, which is fine if you see that it can be beneficial for you. But when you are starting out, no one cares about you until you prove how good you really are. For this reason, I recommend registering with every agent that will accept you on this basis. If you only register with one, you may miss out on something that your agent hasn't been called for. Of course, if you live in an area that only has one agency for models, then you must be satisfied.

After you register with the agencies and sit back to wait for the phone to ring, you may get a little restless if you aren't called right away. The best thing to do is to start to "make the rounds." That is, go directly to the people who hire models. It is time-consuming, but you don't have to see everyone; just schedule your interviews so that they make you feel like you are doing something about your career without taking up all of your leisure time.

Again, consult the yellow pages of the telephone directory. These are the headings of the people who use models:
- 1.   Commercial Photographers
- 2.   Motion Picture Producers
- 3.   Women's Apparel Manufacturers
- 4.   Department Stores (ask for the Fashion Department)
- 5.   Advertising Agencies

There may be other places, too, but this will give you more than enough to work on. If you have enough composites, say 500 or 1000, you can mail your photos out to these people and only actually see a handful of them in person to save yourself some time. If you can't afford to hand out a large number of photos or composites, then be selective about whom you go and see. Always call first and make an appointment. Don't ever just "drop in." Some places will not see models for an interview and deal only with an advertising agency. By calling first, you eliminate those that are not interested in you, and you avoid wasting your photographs on these people.

Wear a dress, hose and heels when you go for your interview, and be as well-groomed as you possibly can. Remember that good carriage and posture are requisites for every model. Unless you are going for an interview for a fashion show, no one is going to ask you to walk or do fancy pivots. In most cases you will be hired because you look like the girl they visualized when they laid out their advertising campaign. You don't have to be perfect to be a model, but you must be unique in your own way.

A good example is Lauren Hutton, who is now a movie star. Lauren is 5' 7½" tall, with dark blonde hair, and weighs 118 pounds. Her cheekbones are rather high, but her eyes are slightly crossed and she has a wide gap between her two front teeth. Lauren signed a contract with Charles Revson, when she was 29 years old, to promote his Ultima II cosmetics. The contract called for her to get $200,000 a year for the first two years, with an escalated scale after that. She's made a number of films, but we still see her face in the pages of fashion magazines selling cosmetics. In the beginning, they told her she'd never make it. She was an ex-Playboy Bunny and not at all like the flat-chested, toothpick-thin models everyone was hiring. Eileen Ford even suggested to Lauren that she get her teeth capped and fix her nose before she could work as a model, but somehow Lauren never got around to it. Yes, Lauren was and is unique.

So you must never be discouraged. Allow yourself at least one year to find out whether you will be suitable for this type of work. You will very seldom get an immediate break. Just remember, if you get that first job, one job somehow leads to another and another. Soon people will be calling you, instead of you nagging them for work. Word gets around if you are good. (It gets around if you are difficult to work with, too.)

When you decide to "break into" this business, you do not need to ask any "experts" if they think you can make it. No one can tell you this. This is evident by the many types of models who have already made it big. You might be that special person who can do it, too. The worst that can happen is that you'll have an interesting time while you're finding out, and you'll have some novel things to write in your diary. Just consider it another one of life's adventures. Enjoy what you can. Enjoy your new beautiful body in every way that you can. That way you'll never ever want to let it go.

Desirable Weights for Men

(without clothes)

Height (without shoes)	Small	Average	Large
5′ 3″	118	129	141
5′ 4″	122	133	145
5′ 5″	126	137	149
5′ 6″	130	142	155
5′ 7″	134	147	161
5′ 8″	139	151	166
5′ 9″	143	155	170
5′ 10″	147	159	174
5′ 11″	150	163	178
6′	154	167	183
6′ 1″	158	171	188
6′ 2″	162	175	192
6′ 3″	165	178	195
6′ 4″	170	181	199
6′ 5″	175	186	203

Desirable Weights for Women

(without clothes)

Height (without shoes)	Small	Average	Large
4′ 9″	95	102	112
4′ 10″	96	104	114
4′ 11″	98	106	116
5′	100	109	118
5′ 1″	104	112	121
5′ 2″	107	115	125
5′ 3″	110	118	128
5′ 4″	113	122	132
5′ 5″	116	125	135
5′ 6″	120	129	139
5′ 7″	123	132	142
5′ 8″	126	136	146
5′ 9″	130	140	150
5′ 10″	133	144	156
5′ 11″	137	148	161
6′	141	152	166

Index